Resources for Language
and Area Studies

FRED C. SCHATZ
Academic Dean

COMMITTEE ON LANGUAGE AND AREA CENTERS

Appointed by the American Council on Education

E. *Wilson Lyon*
President, Pomona College; *Chairman*

Y. R. *Chao*
Professor of Oriental Languages, University of California, Berkeley

Peter Elder
Dean, Graduate School of Arts and Sciences, Harvard University

Gerard J. Mangone
Director of Overseas Training Program, Maxwell Graduate School
of Citizenship and Public Affairs, Syracuse University

Ruth Mulhauser
Professor of Romance Languages, Western Reserve University

Charles E. Odegaard
President, University of Washington

Rev. Walter J. Ong, S.J.
Professor of English, Saint Louis University

———————

Harrison Sasscer
Staff Associate, American Council on Education; *Secretary*

RESOURCES FOR LANGUAGE AND AREA STUDIES

A REPORT ON AN INVENTORY
OF THE LANGUAGE AND AREA CENTERS
SUPPORTED BY THE NATIONAL DEFENSE
EDUCATION ACT OF 1958

JOSEPH AXELROD *and*
DONALD N. BIGELOW

AMERICAN COUNCIL ON EDUCATION · *Washington, D,C,*

PROJECT STAFF

JOSEPH AXELROD, *Director*

DONALD N. BIGELOW, *Associate Director*

HERMAN R. ALLEN

HANS HAINEBACH

MARTHE REXROTH

The research reported herein was performed pursuant to a
contract with the Office of Education, U.S. Department of
Health, Education, and Welfare.

Foreword

O NE OF THE primary purposes of the National Defense Education Act of 1958 was to stimulate the study of modern foreign languages. The results of this stimulation have been most readily apparent in the installation of language laboratories in secondary schools and in the provision of summer institutes for language teachers. Less apparent, but no less important, has been the impact of the National Defense Education Act on the study of languages heretofore rarely taught in American colleges and universities or, in some instances, not taught at all prior to 1958. With the assistance of funds available under title VI of the National Defense Education Act, forty-six centers for the study of critically needed but infrequently taught languages were in operation by the academic year 1960–61.

At the request of the Language Development Section of the U.S. Office of Education, the American Council on Education accepted a contract to make an inventory of the forty-six language and area centers which would bring together information on how the centers were organized, the number of students enrolled in language and area disciplines, the method of teaching languages, and the relation between language and area studies. The Council undertook this service for the Office of Education with the full understanding that the inventory would be descriptive rather than evaluative. In all likelihood, the information developed through this inventory will become the basis for evaluation of the work of the centers and indeed of the entire center program. In view of the fact that these centers are located at colleges and universities which are member institutions of the Council, such an evaluation can be more appropriately made by an agency other than the Council.

The fact that this inventory is primarily descriptive does not diminish the significance of its findings. In this revision of what was

[v]

submitted to the Office of Education as a detailed technical report is told the story of an important development in the relationships between the Federal Government and higher education. Through the language and area center program the Federal Government has provided substantial direct support for the first time on a large scale to disciplines that traditionally are regarded as belonging to the humanities rather than to the sciences. Moreover, as this inventory shows, the Federal Government has provided its share of the financing of language and area centers without impairing the autonomy of the institutions receiving the funds; in short, federal funds have been given without federal control.

In publishing this study the Council hopes to reach a wider audience than specialists in language and area studies. College and university administrators, foundation and governmental executives, members of Congress and of state legislatures, and concerned members of the general public will want to consider the implications of the program described in this inventory. As the authors have pointed out, there must be a planned and orderly future development of language and area studies. If this document proves useful to those who participate in planning the future of language and area studies in the United States, it will have served its purpose well.

On behalf of the Council I wish to thank the authors of this report, Dr. Joseph Axelrod and Dr. Donald N. Bigelow, for producing a trenchant and informative document. I join with the authors in thanking the other members of the Inventory staff whose detailed reports on individual centers provided the raw material for this final and summary report. The Council is especially appreciative of the diligence with which the members of the Committee on Language and Area Centers attended meetings of the committee and submitted comments on the various drafts of the inventory report.

Finally, special acknowledgment is owed to Arthur S. Adams who, as my predecessor in office, committed the Council to an undertaking of which this document is the end product. As in so many things related to the Council, we are all indebted to his foresight.

LOGAN WILSON, *President,*
American Council on Education

Preface

FEDERAL FUNDS FOR THE humanities represent a radical departure in the history of American higher education. Under the National Defense Education Act of 1958, among other provisions, the humanities, specifically language instruction, were given unique encouragement whereby, with matching funds, the Federal Government and some thirty universities have cooperated in establishing forty-six language and area centers in the United States.[1]

This is the final report of an inventory of these centers by the American Council on Education during the academic year 1960–61. Such action was needed because of the significance of this joint enterprise between the Office of Education and American universities and colleges. Also, because there was already available a great deal of information which had been neither collected nor analyzed, it seemed appropriate to make such an inventory at this time.

Although the 1958 legislation has been extended through June 1964,[2] it is hoped that any future action can be taken with as full knowledge as possible of what has happened at the centers. By the fall of 1960, nineteen centers were in their second year of operation and twenty-seven were beginning their first year of work. In view of the 1958 law's relatively short duration (four years), an inventory taken in 1960–61 could hardly be thought premature.

Each of the forty-six centers was visited by one or more of the staff of four visitors—Herman R. Allen and Hans Hainebach, in addition to ourselves—and every attempt was made to take an individual in-

[1] A forty-seventh center was added after our inventory was taken, and five new Latin American centers were named in December 1961, while this report was in press.
[2] Thus, financial aid for NDEA centers is now assured until the close of the 1964–65 academic year.

ventory without making comparative evaluations. For each center one person was responsible for writing the inventory.

The present report is based on these forty-six separate inventories and on the discussions which took place at five regional conferences, for which separate reports were also written. These conferences were held under the auspices of the American Council on Education during the spring of 1961, after the visits had been completed. Here group discussions (on a specific world region) augmented, synthesized, and often helped to explain the information previously obtained on an individual basis. Altogether a total of fifty-one reports were written and, notwithstanding a desire for brevity, they contain something over a half million words.

These reports are on file with the Language Development Section of the Office of Education in the Department of Health, Education, and Welfare, and are available to its personnel for study as well as to others to whom the Office has had copies sent.

The present report is divided into three chapters, none of which stands alone. The progression from one to the next moves simultaneously on two planes: from past to present to future, and from conceptual to concrete to problematical. Nonetheless, chapter 2, "Current Resources and Practices," remains the heart of the report, since it attempts to condense in general terms what was found in the forty-six, usually quite different, centers. Of necessity it is the most detailed and the most descriptive. Some of the information included in it is already obsolete in view of the fact that the inventory was taken during the autumn semester of 1960–61. The significance of this chapter, however, emerges when it is read in relationship to the one that precedes and the one that follows it.

Since the object of this final report is to present a composite picture, usually no particular center is identified in the passages cited from the reports on file at the Office of Education. Wherever possible, we have eschewed scholarly dots and brackets in the interest of smoothness of reading. In addition, "this center," "the center director," and other such terms are generally substituted for specific names in passages actually quoted from our inventories. The passages quoted are meant, of course, only to illustrate generalizations which the sum of our experience during 1960–61 seemed to warrant.

The director and associate director of the project have worked together closely since September 1960. This is their joint report, the product of a year's deliberations. The associate director is responsible for chapter 1; the director is responsible for chapter 2; and chapter 3 was written jointly by them. The appendices were prepared by the director.

In spite of the hurricane in the fall of 1960, the blizzard in February, and the subsequent beautiful spring in Washington—which were the times the Committee on Language and Area Centers chose to meet—nature did not interrupt the committee's helpfulness to us. We wish to express our appreciation, too, to the directors and acting directors of the forty-six centers who were, almost to a man, willing and able to provide us with the information that is the stuff of the center inventories.

The Language Development Section of the Office of Education made available its files to the Council and gave assistance whenever it was needed. Arthur S. Adams, president of the American Council on Education during most of the project's existence, and Harrison Sasscer, the member of the Council's staff assigned to work directly with the project, deserve special mention for helping to bridge the gap of the human vagaries and many miles which separated San Francisco from Washington, D.C. And, at the project headquarters in San Francisco, many technical problems in the production of the inventories as well as of this final report were solved by the ever-willing and capable Ida Hodes and John Warner. To Marthe Rexroth, administrative assistant for the project, we owe more than we can say.

In view of the importance of the problem of how to teach modern foreign languages, appreciation must be expressed to Y. R. Chao, of the University of California; George Faust, of the University of Kentucky; Albert Marckwardt, of the University of Michigan; and others for reading and making suggestions concerning the early drafts of Appendix A, "The Audio-lingual Approach in College and University Language Teaching."

Finally, we appreciate the many comments that have come to us from readers of the preliminary edition, which appeared in August 1961. On the basis of these suggestions, chapters 1 and 3 have been considerably revised.

J.A.
D.N.B.

Contents

List of Tables

CHAPTER 1

The Center Concept

THE CONCEPT OF A LANGUAGE and area center is a new and pervasive force in American higher education. Except for the recent spurt of activity in the natural sciences, nothing in recent years has made such an impact on the liberal arts colleges and graduate schools. And the impact is greater because the hope, as always, lies in the humanities and in man himself, in what he creates and, significantly, in how he communicates.

The center concept may well be a new turn of the wheel destined to upset the academic apple cart. Now, for the first time since the teachers of Latin, Greek, and mathematics dominated the college curriculum a century ago, another trio has come together with a common purpose other than just to teach. The humanist, the social scientist, and the historian are jointly involved in a common educational program known as "language and area centers."

The center concept combines the study of the rarely, or uncommonly, taught languages of the world with more and more course work in those non-Western civilizations that speak the languages. It emphasizes the new and vital interest higher education has in the world's civilizations heretofore dismissed as inferior or unimportant or, what has often been the case, as possessing "no worthwhile literature." The present need to communicate immediately with almost everyone has again drawn attention to the dangerous academic barriers of intellectual aloofness and cultural snobbishness. To date, language and area centers have so successfully challenged the colleges' traditional preoccupation with Western civilization that it is now appropriate to claim equal rights for all civilizations.

While the National Defense Education Act of 1958 had nothing to do with starting the notion of language and area centers, it effectively dramatized the development of the center concept—to which it gave new meaning and added strength—on a national scale. It brought the prestige of the government to a matter of vital importance. And with the use of matching funds it has materially assisted in the growth of these programs in American universities across the country. Not only has the operation been carried out with great success; it has also proceeded without the slightest indication of government interference.

The National Defense Education Act of 1958 specifies that in addition to the study of the modern foreign languages which are considered critical, and for which adequate instruction is not available, the centers may give instruction "in other fields needed to provide a full understanding of the areas, regions, or countries in which such language is commonly used . . . , including fields such as history, political science, linguistics, economics, sociology, geography, and anthropology." (Public Law 85-864, section 601a.) Beyond this statement, however, there was no directive regarding the shape these centers should take. The goals themselves could have been fulfilled by various kinds of centers—for there were many models—and could have been created on the basis of quite different center concepts. An initial problem was the word "establishment," and the Office of Education had to decide immediately whether "to establish" meant to establish something new or to support something already in existence. This was one of several basic problems facing the Office of Education in determining how the centers could properly and legally be established. At the same time certain conditions helped to predetermine, at least in part, the course of action finally decided upon, and some of them are discussed below.

Once the Language Development Section of the Office of Education was organized and the various problems considered, a general understanding of what constitutes a "center" emerged—but not all at once. The shape of the concept was clear enough, however, during the early months of operation so that a beginning could be made, and nineteen centers were quickly established. But the center concept was not then or subsequently ever formally delineated. It has been and is still continually evolving.

A large number of centers were already in operation all over the country, each different from the other. The Office of Education decided to help support many of them and, at the same time, to help organize some quite new centers as well. Those already in existence remained essentially unchanged except that new or expanded activities were added to the original program. From the very beginning, the Office dealt with each center on its own terms, recognizing the right of a center to self-determination. As a result, the center concept, always somewhat flexible, was not subsequently defined with any greater preciseness.

The Genesis of the Concept

Early efforts in the development of the language and area center concept go back to the First World War. For instance, the University of Texas had one of the first area programs to be organized at any American university; a 1915 bulletin of that institution lists courses "for the study of Latin America." At the second Pan-American Scientific Congress, held in December 1916, the suggestion was made that Spanish be taught from the point of view of Latin-American customs. And, indeed, Latin America became the first region of the world to which the area approach was applied, an approach that foreshadowed the center concept as it was to be used by many institutions for other regions of the world.

After the First World War, Columbia College started its now famous contemporary civilization course which, although dealing only with Western civilization, was a basic move in the construction of area courses demanding the interrelationship of several disciplines to a given world region. In his annual report for 1918, President Nicholas Murray Butler of Columbia University stated that "the chief purpose in studying French should be to gain an understanding and appreciation of France," and this statement, too, gave recognition to the notion of area *and* language programs. During the 1920's and 1930's, Latin American area programs continued to increase, only to decline sharply after the Second World War.

Meanwhile, however, there was another and quite independent attempt to apply the language and area mold (the center concept) to other regions of the world. The idea that it was desirable to supplant the single scholar in a non-Western civilization by a group of specialists was being expressed in several ways and by some people. This idea remains the core of the concept.

During these formative years, to take quite different men, all of whom approached the problem quite differently, W. Norman Brown of the University of Pennsylvania, Raymond A. Kennedy of Yale University, and Philip Khuri Hitti of Princeton University, among others, did pioneer work in creating an interest in the center concept. These teachers represented different disciplines and different world areas but they were all headed toward the same goal which was, ultimately, to teach a modern foreign language with comprehensive area instruction at the same time. Some had the goal clearly in mind; others were unknowingly moving in this direction.

Early efforts placed the emphasis on area. Hitti claimed there was need for adequate university-level instruction on Islam and, although a classicist, he stressed the modern world in the Middle East. Kennedy, an anthropologist who was killed in Indonesia while on a scientific field mission of consequence to area research, was one of the first to see the possibilities of teaching the area known as Southeast Asia. And more continuously than many of the others, W. Norman Brown, professor of Sanskrit since 1926 and chairman of his university's South Asia Regional Studies Program since it was created in 1947, has proceeded in the same direction of his own initial and determined efforts in the field of area studies. In particular, his goal has been to establish area programs along lines in which a team of specialists would replace Sanskritists like himself, and, as much as any one person, he is responsible for the impetus given to the center concept at this time.

Previously, the single scholar in a non-Western field taught everything. He did the work later done by the historian, the geographer, the political scientist, the linguist, and the philosopher. Professor Brown has written:

In the first part of the Twentieth Century, the study of India and adjacent areas was fostered in America at some eight universities and at each lay in the hands of a single person, who was the professor of Sanskrit. His primary interest was classical language and literature . . . and if history was to be taught, he taught it, and so too any art, anthropology, sociology, even economics.[1]

This teacher usually taught only the classical language of his region

---

[1] Private communication from the University of Pennsylvania to the Ford Foundation, dated September 1960.

and was seldom concerned on any scholarly level with the modern spoken language or, indeed, with the modern period of that region.

A notable event took place in the early 1930's when the Committee on Indic and Iranian Studies of the American Council of Learned Societies (ACLS) discussed the idea of studying South Asia by applying "the combined techniques of a number of different intellectual fields." Its deliberations were formally recommended at a conference which met at the University of Pennsylvania in 1934. Five years later, Professor Brown, as chairman of the ACLS Committee on Indic and Iranian Studies, stated that humanistic studies in the West have been largely confined to our own civilization. Professor Brown made a strong case for the study of other civilizations to which more attention should be given, not only to permit us a "wider world-view," but also to enable us to act intelligently in the future. Speaking specifically of the need to develop an Indic studies program in the United States, Professor Brown noted that even though there were teachers of Sanskrit, India itself was virtually unrepresented in any academic department on any campus. A professor of Sanskrit, he said, could hardly be expected to control India's languages, literature, philosophy, "and whatever else may be considered part of a historic culture. We do not expect such universality of a professor of French or German," he concluded, "yet India is no mere France or Germany; it is a whole Europe, with a history even longer."[2]

Brown's case for extending the study of India in American universities was reiterated by others who strove to initiate or expand programs on India and on other similarly neglected world areas. Indeed, there were many who believed it was necessary to criticize an educational enterprise rooted in understanding only Western civilization and in learning a few classical languages. These people, in sum, were the pioneers who helped to push the center concept in the face of academic inertia and public apathy. They were to be greatly assisted by the educational foundations and, more dramatically, by the Second World War, during which time the lack of American scholarly competence in the various regions of the world was all too quickly and too clearly revealed.

For it took the Second World War to drive home the point that

[2] W. Norman Brown, "India and Humanistic Studies in America," *Bulletin of the American Council of Learned Societies,* No. 28, May 1939, pp. 22–23.

the early pioneers in language and area work had been making. Ignorance of cultures other than Western civilization was abysmal. There was no systematic coverage of the areas of the world and there were inadequate facilities for training new personnel. In short, there were but few area-trained scholars on hand. What was worse, few people knew, and fewer still could teach, the modern uncommonly taught languages that were spoken throughout the war-torn world. When it is recalled that until the Second World War most modern language instruction followed the grammar-translation method, that is, almost no attention was given to learning to speak a language, the dismal condition that faced a country at war can be realized.

Some years before the Second World War, the Rockefeller Foundation began to encourage the study of foreign languages. In 1933 the General Education Board awarded its first fellowship in this field. It was for the study of Japanese, as was the second fellowship, which was given in the following year to Edwin Reischauer, who only recently became Ambassador to Japan. In 1934, the foundation gave grants to Columbia, Harvard, and to the Institute of Pacific Relations for instruction in Russian. Three years later, Yale received a grant for Chinese and, in the following year, Columbia was also given one for instruction in the same language. In 1939 Cornell received a grant for Russian and Princeton received one for Turkish.

In those years before the Second World War, however, no single grant of the Rockefeller Foundation had as great an influence on language training as the one (the first of nine) made to the American Council of Learned Societies. This was awarded in 1941, before the United States entered the war, and was intended to provide instruction in the neglected modern foreign languages which might be needed by the country's Armed Forces; French, Spanish, German, and Italian were specifically excluded. From this emergency intensive language program there was obtained the experience which was to prove indispensable in the subsequent creation and development of the Army Specialized Training Program (ASTP).

Even before the ACLS intensive language program began, Dr. Mortimer Graves, administrative secretary of the ACLS, had, through his reports, speeches, and articles, done much to spur interest in language training, so fundamental to the center concept. That his efforts were successful can be seen by a conference which he and Dr.

J. Milton Cowan, director of the ACLS program (and another pioneer in the field), held in Chicago, March 1943. This conference attempted "to formulate a curriculum in language and area studies for the Army" to which representatives of twelve universities were invited.[3]

Edward Sapir and Leonard Bloomfield, both disciples of Franz Boas, had made significant contributions to linguistics, and the latter certainly influenced the principles and methods of teaching used in the ACLS program. The important point to note here is that the scholar played a direct role in the development of this program that subsequently was to influence the ASTP to such a large degree. Furthermore, and of equal significance, the ASTP did not prescribe the methods to be used when teaching foreign languages but only made recommendations based on the intensive language program of ACLS.

The history of the Army Specialized Training Program is told elsewhere,[4] and its significance in the development of the language and area programs of the 1960's should not be underestimated, although it is often misrepresented and exaggerated. The connection between those early pioneers, the ACLS program and the ASTP, was not a tenuous one. The imagination that was shown by the ASTP was largely the outcome of the thinking of those same scholars who had previously been concerned with the early center concept in its various phases. In addition, some of those pioneers, and others interested in language and area work, were in Washington during the first hectic years of the war and their story is still to be told. The attempt to recruit personnel by government agencies during the war is a dramatic one, and the trials of the unprepared scholars called to service undoubtedly play a larger role in the creation of the center concept than is currently realized. Certainly there were many diverse influences at work. The list of these scholars is long, and includes W. Norman Brown from Pennsylvania, John W. Gardner of the Carnegie Corporation, C. B. Fahs of the Rockefeller Foundation, George Taylor of the University of Washington, and many, many others.

In any case the Army Specialized Training Program in area and language work began in April 1943, and by December of that year,

[3] Alfonse Ralph Miele, "Armed Forces Language Training in Peacetime" (Unpublished dissertation, Columbia University, 1958), p. 4.

[4] Robert John Matthew, *Language and Area Studies in the Armed Forces* (Washington: American Council on Education, 1947).

fifty-five institutions had a total enrollment of 13,185 students. All of them acquired some skill in speaking a foreign language and, in addition, were taught something of the area's recent history, its geography, and so forth. The so-called "army system" worked. The concept was launched. In spite of the highly experimental nature of the venture and the fact that it lasted but one year, it did kindle the imagination of many teachers and helped demonstrate the potentialities of the center concept for postwar education. Not only did ASTP help to devise new methods of teaching a foreign language (involving intensive work utilizing daily drill and informants), but it also showed that language teaching could and should be coordinated with the teaching of the various disciplines concerned with a given area of the world. The ASTP was the first major application of the science of linguistics to language teaching. Most important of all, perhaps, the ASTP units helped to develop the personnel for the work the universities were to do at the war's end.

After 1945 language and area centers grew rapidly, and the scholarly world began to take notice of what was happening. The Social Science Research Council's Committee on World Area Research sponsored two surveys of area facilities in American universities. The first was prepared in 1946[5] and the second, edited by Wendell C. Bennett, in 1951.[6] The latter revealed a reasonable success in some twenty-nine programs and indicated that in the intervening five years the number of such programs had doubled. In 1954, when a third basic report on area study programs appeared (prepared by the State Department),[7] it was announced that there were some sixty-two language and area programs in operation. That report applied the same criteria used by Professor Bennett. All reports indicated that this rapid growth would not have occurred if it had not been for the substantial foundation support given the universities. Between 1945 and 1948, according to this third report, the various foundations gave many millions of dollars for area training and research programs. In 1956 some eighty-one programs were counted, and by

[5] Robert B. Hall, *Area Studies,* Social Science Research Council Pamphlet 3 (New York: The Council, 1947).

[6] Bennett (ed.), *Area Studies in American Universities* (New York: Social Science Research Council, 1951).

[7] *Area Study Programs in American Universities* (Washington: External Research Division, Bureau of Intelligence and Research, Dept. of State, 1954).

1959 there were ninety-six area study programs in American universities.[8] Interestingly enough, there were more programs in Latin America tabulated than in any other world region. Programs dealing with Russia and Eastern Europe were not a very close second.

Since a detailed listing of foundation grants would be cumbersome here, and the information may be found in the annual reports of the foundations, only some indication of what was done is needed. During the war years, for instance, the Rockefeller Foundation continued its support of languages. Between 1940 and 1957, the American Council of Learned Societies received a total of $245,000, the first $50,000 of which helped to start the ACLS intensive language program already referred to. For the period 1942–48 the University of California was given $246,325 in some seven grants. Harvard, for 1943–55, received three grants totaling $105,000. The University of Pennsylvania was given $69,500 between 1943 and 1947; and the University of Chicago, for the period 1944–48, received $104,600. Between 1944 and 1954 the Modern Language Association (MLA) received altogether five grants, for a total of $244,000.

The grants made by the Carnegie Corporation were also extensive and important. For example, the University of Michigan received $350,000 for its Japanese area study center; Yale received two five-year grants, beginning in 1946, of $150,000 each for its Southeast Asia program; Princeton received two grants of $61,500 each for its Near East program; in 1947 Pennsylvania received a grant for $155,000, another, in 1952, for $150,000, and a third, in 1957, for $85,000, in order to expand its South Asia program. One of the most valuable of all the grants made by Carnegie was a related grant to area study under which the Social Science Research Council received $800,000 for fellowships, which were generally given for work in anthropology, international relations, sociology, and other area subjects, but *not* for language study.

Any attempt to itemize the various projects in international training and research sponsored by the Ford Foundation would be quite difficult. Beginning in 1951 and continuing through to the present time, when grants in the millions are being made for area programs,

[8] Reports for 1956 and 1959 were each issued under the title *Area Study Programs in American Universities* (Washington: External Research Division, Bureau of Intelligence and Research, Dept. of State, 1956, 1959).

the Ford grants cover foreign area programs, language training, fellowships, research, publications, and assistance to libraries. Without any doubt the foundation has played a vital role in helping to make area studies a permanent part of many universities. Its first major grant was a $480,000 foundation-administered project for fellowships to Asia and the Near and Middle East in 1952; the next one was a $100,000 grant to the University of Michigan and an additional $500,000 the next year, made for its program of study on the Near East. In 1953 Columbia received $150,000 for a three-year program in Near and Middle East Studies. During the next two years, the Ford Foundation made substantial grants to Boston University and to Northwestern University for programs on Africa. And in 1955 they gave $500,000 to Cornell University for its program in foreign rural extension education. But this, too, is only a sample of foundation support and indicates only part of what occurred in the first decade after the war.

What the war did on one level, the foundations did on another, and both materially gave the center concept new meaning as well as greater reality. It must be noted that the significance of the money granted is out of all proportion to the amounts involved since most universities would have had no center programs had they not been subsidized.

The story of the battle to strike a balance between area work and language training at the centers is a tangled one, with a good deal of academic narrowness of view running throughout. Centers oriented in the direction of the social sciences often failed to give language its due, and vice versa. In addition, language-oriented centers sometimes failed to recognize the importance of the other humanistic disciplines. In some instances, outside influences reflected the same prejudices that were found on campus, and it was not always easy to start a center with a proper balance between language *and* area.

Thus, the concept of a language and area center was being applied on many campuses in many different ways, according to local talent and local situations. While the international demands upon the universities grew and some universities themselves offered other proposals to students to encourage them to go abroad, under one guise or another, to learn to speak another language, at base the center concept remained intellectually sound and modestly ambitious with the long-range, academic goals always in mind. By 1959 there were almost a hundred programs of graduate study of foreign areas in some fifty universities—and this was exclusive of any of the new programs that were established under title VI of the National Defense Education Act.

During the 1950's a climate of opinion in the academic world favorable to language and area programs for non-Western civilizations could be said to have existed; but it was not predominant. Undergraduate general education courses were helping in this direction; but language training, as such, remained weak. Still, enough work in language had been done and enough language and area development had actually occurred to give respectability to this kind of a program on many campuses. The increased concern of American higher education in international matters, however sporadic and unplanned, became a contributing factor in the growing stability and acceptance of the center concept.

There is no need here to trace the passage of the legislation known as the National Defense Education Act of 1958 since this chapter is concerned only with the growth of the center concept. It must be indicated, however, that the Modern Language Association, in its own concern with the development of more "modern" methods of teaching foreign languages, influenced both the center concept *and* the passage of the NDEA. And, of course, the act itself altered the concept still further.

The influence of the Foreign Language Program of the MLA on language training in general and the NDEA in particular is complex and crucial. No other professional group has played so important a role. The leadership of William R. Parker, professor of English at Indiana University, has been widely recognized.[9] As executive secretary of the MLA from 1947 to 1955, Parker directed the project to inquire into the role which foreign languages should play in American life, a project to which the Rockefeller Foundation gave $120,000 in 1952 and, two years later, an additional $115,000.

The condition which the MLA was seeking to improve—a condition which beset all foreign language teaching in this country—was grave. A vast majority of the language teachers in American schools and colleges were not closely acquainted with the new materials and

---

[9] He is the author of the significant policy document, *The National Interest and Foreign Languages,* a Department of State publication (6389), released in January 1957, sponsored by the U.S. National Commission for Unesco. A revision of this pamphlet is in preparation.

methods for teaching languages that had been developed during the war and postwar period. Their knowledge of these materials was usually limited to a second-hand or third-hand description of them. But even if they had been closely acquainted with them, most of the teachers did not have the linguistic or pedagogic skills required to put these new methods into successful operation, however great their will might have been. Moreover, even if they had had the will, the knowledge, and the skills which the task demanded, they would not have received from their superiors the necessary encouragement or the physical facilities necessary to the success of the new methods.

The years immediately preceding the passage of the National Defense Education Act were crucial. The concept of area studies, academically inspired, given focus by the war and support by the foundations, was becoming firmer. The Modern Language Association was doubling its efforts in combating the woeful inadequacy of the conditions and methods of language instruction in the United States.[10] The Office of Education's report on Soviet education appeared.[11] Legislation foreshadowing the language provisions of the National Defense Education Act was in draft form before Sputnik presented the challenge which did so much to bring together all these previous efforts so that, finally, the national emergency with respect to second-language mastery became generally acknowledged. And the language title of the act —title VI—came into being.

The Elements of the Concept

Title VI of the National Defense Education Act authorized the *establishment* of language and area centers. This meant the creation of something new, something which had had no prior existence. But

---

[10] In view of the NDEA, title VI, provision for language and area centers, the following passage from a 1956 MLA policy statement is especially interesting: "We urge the establishment of *centers of instruction* in colleges and universities in various parts of the country, each one specializing in a single group of languages spoken by millions of people but practically unknown to us. It would be desirable also to make available in each center instruction in the geography, history, economics, and politics of the language area studied. It is essential and urgent *educational planning,* regional and national, that we call for . . ." This policy statement originally appeared in *Publications of the Modern Language Association,* September 1956, Part II, under the title "F.L. Program Policy" and was later reprinted in pamphlet form.

[11] *Education in the USSR,* U.S. Office of Education Bulletin 1957, No. 14 (Washington: Government Printing Office, May 1957).

the severe limitation on the supply of experts in the uncommonly taught languages and the underdeveloped areas which existed then (and which, of course, still exists) could not be ignored. These experts were already located on certain campuses where language and area programs—even though some were quite small—already existed. Hence, unless the law were to be interpreted in such a way as to permit support of already existing but newly expanded programs, the Office of Education would simply have been acting on the principle of robbing Peter to pay Paul. What would have been the point of supporting a newly established center at X University, if that program depended upon the recruitment of Y University's staff, who were already working in an existing language and area program?

The decision on the part of Office of Education authorities to support needed activities in language and area which were *new*, whether or not they were initial activities in a newly established center or expanded activities in an already existing enterprise, was the most crucial single decision rendered. This decision stimulated expansion in the following directions on those campuses where programs had existed before NDEA: (*a*) developing intensive language courses, where only non-intensive courses had previously existed; (*b*) expanding the area offerings and encouraging appointments of experts on non-Western areas in each of the relevant disciplines in the fields of history, the behavioral sciences, and the humanities; (*c*) expanding programs upwards to include advanced language and area courses not hitherto given; (*d*) expanding the language program to include other uncommonly taught languages not hitherto offered on the campus. Support from NDEA thus made the concept of area studies, developed in the 1930's, a reality; for it fostered teams of area specialists and it accelerated the expansion of offerings in the languages of the non-Western areas, on a national level and with professional backing.

On many of the larger campuses, the nucleus of a center already existed at the time the act was passed. As has been noted, the Office of Education decided to use what already existed when feasible as the basis for its language and area centers, provided of course that the university was willing to meet at least half the cost of program expansion. But the Language Development Section in no way prescribed the directions of growth which a center was to take. The center itself, if it wished to apply for support from the Federal Government, had the responsibility of working out its own patterns of expansion. The doctrine of "local option"—the center's right to self-determination—prevailed from the beginning.

It goes without saying, of course, that a plan of operation had to be submitted which gave assurance that the center's expanded program would serve the goals designated in title VI. Allowable expenses had to be determined, an acceptable budget drawn up, and the center concept developed independently on each campus, often unrelated to other centers. But the point most basic to the center concept, as it developed, was that no model was supplied by the Office of Education. The framework within which each center was to flourish was to be entirely of its own creation, designed to fit best its own unique conditions and ambitions.

Moreover, because each university structure differs from almost every other, often in basic design and always in its details, there could be no standardizing. None was conceived or desired. Nonetheless, the basic center concept was at work, and the concept itself influenced language development and pushed area studies in several distinct directions.

The most significant of these directions can be described as a kind of interdisciplinary growth. This could not perhaps take place on a few campuses where the individual departments have remained impenetrable bastions of medieval autonomy. But on many campuses, as the language and area centers grew, along with the general courses in non-Western civilizations which were beginning to appear in undergraduate programs, a pattern of departmental cooperation began to emerge. This development demanded not only that the faculty members of all the area disciplines work together, but that the faculty in language and the faculty in area work hand in hand as well.

The likelihood is that without the NDEA centers, the degree of interdepartmental cooperation which took place on many campuses would not have occurred as rapidly as it did—and in a few cases, as our reports indicated, such cooperation might perhaps not have come into being at all without the assistance given to such development by the NDEA center.

By and large, the center concept focused attention on the instruction of students in graduate standing, since it was on that level where most of the work in the uncommonly taught languages was carried on. And support was needed on this level, it was felt, if undergraduate programs were eventually to be affected. The hypothesis supporting this view was a simple one: the graduate schools would begin to produce the Ph.D.'s in language and area who would then fill teaching posts at the college level.

However, external forces again influenced the direction of the program. Because the elementary courses in the critical languages either were offered through the undergraduate division of the university or were open to all students, undergraduate as well as graduate, greater exposure on the undergraduate level to the new programs took place more quickly than had originally been envisaged. While this is now already a common situation for languages such as Japanese and Chinese, it was Russian which, of course, led this movement downward to undergraduate instruction.

On the area side, the undergraduate program had already been affected through the introduction of general courses on non-Western civilizations, and that development, too, began independently of the instruction in the uncommonly taught languages. The NDEA center, however, has served to bring together these two quite different types of instruction.

The center concept can no longer be said to be a local matter; it has entered the national scene, not only because of the National Defense Education Act but because of its significance to higher education itself. The very notion of the center concept carries with it a desire to achieve certain aims beyond those of formal education. It has helped to bring into focus national needs and private scholarship. It has shown scholars the urgency of pooling resources in teaching as well as in research.

Meanwhile, the center concept becomes clearer. The search for an equilibrium such as this must be the story of all centers: *Surely a model center would study a geographical area without confusing it with an academic discipline, would consider language basic to such a study, would acquire interdisciplinary mobility while maintaining its own identity, and would assert its own unity of purpose without sacrificing individual scholarship. While such a center may concentrate on graduate work, it is not restricted to it.* Indeed, the educational system awaits, and needs, the application and force of such a concept.

CHAPTER 2

Current Resources and Practices

THE TERM "CENTER" on college and university campuses normally refers to an administrative unit especially established with the purpose of encouraging and coordinating teaching and research programs on a subject of common interest among a group of faculty members working in various disciplines. This definition does not of course limit itself to the centers included in our inventory. In a language and area center, the teaching and research programs all focus on a given geographic area, including the languages used by its inhabitants.

Center Organization and Administration

On some campuses, such centers are primarily research-oriented. But in the case of the NDEA language and area centers, the focus is on the instructional program. The forty-six centers covered by this inventory offered over 1,200 courses during the autumn semester 1960. Of these, about 550 were courses in more than forty languages, in which almost 7,000 students were enrolled. The centers were staffed by over 600 faculty members, 305 in language and 308 in area studies.

The size of the centers varied greatly: at the smallest, only four students were enrolled in the language courses; at the largest, almost 700 were enrolled in the language courses. Given the differences in size, our visitors expected to find quite different organizational patterns among the centers, even on those campuses which have similar administrative structures. This, in fact, proved to be the case. The relationship between the NDEA center and departments, institutes, and other administrative units on the same campus varied greatly.

A college or university department normally covers only a single discipline. Yet our visitors found some departments at some institutions which were interdisciplinary; on these campuses, they sometimes discovered that the NDEA center has departmental status. For the most part, as will be shown presently, a center is something both more and less than an academic department. The same holds true of its relations to an institute. The term "institute" generally refers to an instructional program, given outside any single department, that yields a certificate rather than a degree. Sometimes, when such an institute offers a language and area program, it is also an NDEA center. In other cases, the institute offers only an area program and is a part of the NDEA center; or, again, the institute may contain the NDEA center within itself as one of its constituent units.

The NDEA centers are not always called "centers" on their home campuses. If the center is itself a department or if it is identical with one of the university institutes, the word "center" is not normally used at the host institution. Center names are, therefore, not uniform, for example, "Chinese-Japanese Language and Area Center," "Southeast Asia Studies," "Middle East Studies Center," "The Institute of Contemporary Russian Studies."

Our data on the centers suggest that the most fruitful analysis of their organization and administration begins by classifying together those centers which find the core of their program in a language department. Sixteen of the forty-six centers (35 percent) are in this category.

At these sixteen centers, the language and literature staff constitutes the whole or the bulk of the center staff, and the language and literature courses constitute the whole or the bulk of the center offerings. In three of these sixteen cases, the language and literature courses that are the core of the center do not constitute a separate department but are attached, by courtesy as it were, to the department of linguistics or to a language department covering a different geographical area. Generally at centers in this category the chairman of the language department is the center director. Often such a director feels his jurisdiction does not go beyond his own department. For example, one of our inventory reports states that the center director, a language department chairman, has no formal control over area courses whatsoever. "Personally," this director told our visitor, "I prefer to let it go at that. My chief job is to promote language and literature in the university and I do what I can to induce students to enroll in well-balanced courses in area work."

Thirty centers (or 65 percent) do not find their program core in a language department. These can be divided into two types: Twenty-five centers (55 percent of the total number) are tightly or loosely organized as interdepartmental enterprises. They include work in language but they have a stronger orientation toward area studies. Five centers (10 percent) reside in a single department or departmentlike unit that is interdisciplinary in nature and that gives course offerings in both language and area.

One of these five centers was described as follows by our visitor: "It provides all of the instruction at the university directly concerned with Russia. Its faculty members belong to no other department and no other department offers course work directly dealing with Russia." Our visitor adds the observation: "The usual problem of working through other departmental chairmen does not exist at this center, since it provides all of its own language and area faculty."

In a second case, the center consists of an interdisciplinary institute and a language department; but these were considered in the present classification as a single entity as they are both headed by the same individual, and our visitor reported that in actual practice they "work together as a single unit."

At the twenty-one centers (45 percent) that are not essentially interdepartmental units, there is, as has already been pointed out, no communication problem among departments. However, at the twenty-five centers (55 percent) that are interdepartmental in their nature, the communication problem has become important and sometimes difficult. One reason for its importance lies in the center's function as a coordinating agency.[1] Indeed, one center director, speaking at

---

[1] During the spring semester 1961, the project director arranged five three-day conferences of language and area center representatives to discuss problems that were revealed by the inventory and to identify practices that were most successful. The five study conferences comprised the following groupings: (1) the Far East, 13 centers; (2) the Near and Middle East, 8 centers; (3) South Asia and Southeast Asia, 10 centers; (4) the Slavic area and East Europe, 11 centers; (5) Africa and the Luso-Brazilian area, 6 centers. (The number exceeds 46 since three centers fall into two different world regions.) Two representatives from each center attended, one for the language side of the center and one for the area side. A listing of the participants at each conference may be found in Appendix C.

A detailed report of each of these conferences was prepared by the project director and submitted to the Language Development Section, U.S. Office of Education.

Conference II, described it as a center's most important function. This director indicated that his center had introduced no new academic degree or program but that it had served to augment, coordinate, and intensify programs already in existence. While no new area degree was introduced, he went on to say, new staff were hired, new ideas were implemented, new interdepartmental programs were introduced; and the result was that individual departmental programs were also greatly enriched.

In some cases, a center became established as an interdepartmental unit because, as one of our visitors reported, "it was not welcome within traditional departments." Occasionally, tension between the center and established departments became unavoidable. But our data also show that when tension between language staff and area staff existed before a center came into existence, the establishment of the center itself, if the director is capable, can become the means of encouraging cooperation. One of our visitors reported, for example: "The center director's personal leadership promises to have a salutary effect in bringing together largely separated activities, namely, instruction in language and literature and instruction in the social sciences and history. At least there is now *some* hope here."

DEGREE AND CERTIFICATE PROGRAMS
FOR GRADUATE STUDENTS

Our data reveal a wide range of patterns in the programs leading to graduate degrees available through the centers or through administrative units with which the centers are formally connected. The programs fall into five categories:

1. A traditional degree program in language and literature, pursued by the center student through the language department.
2. A traditional departmental program in history or in a discipline in the social sciences or in the humanities, but with specialization in a given world area. This is the type of program which discipline-focused students take, for whom the area provides the research site. Such students may not be particularly interested in aspects of area outside their own discipline, although most centers actively encourage the broadening of center-student interests.
3. A departmental program in a particular discipline, with specialization in a given world area and under the guidance of an inter-

departmental committee. This type of program is designed for both discipline-focused students, for whom the area provides the research site, and area-focused students, for whom a discipline provides the research methodology.

4. A program like the preceding, but with the work in area more formally organized by the center, leading either to a joint degree or to a degree in the discipline and a certificate in the area.

5. An interdisciplinary degree program taken directly through the center. In such cases the center may be a department, or it may be departmentlike in its authority to grant degrees.

If we count all five of these program types together, our inventory data show that there were over 1,400 graduate students in such degree and certificate programs at the forty-six centers in the fall semester 1960. Actually, there were almost 2,000 students in such programs if we include also those in major and minor programs for the B.A. degree and special nondegree students (for example, postdoctoral students). A further breakdown of these figures by world area is found in Table 15 of Appendix B (page 92).

The emphasis on interdisciplinary work in the centers is reflected in the number of centers where interdisciplinary degree and certificate programs (the last two types described above) are available. Of the forty-two graduate NDEA language and area centers, thirty-one (or 75 percent) have an interdisciplinary degree program or certificate program available on the graduate level. Ten centers (or just under 25 percent) have available an interdisciplinary Ph.D. degree *major* program; and at six additional centers, where such a major program is not available, an interdisciplinary program *is* available to graduate students as a minor or as part of a program leading to a joint degree—in a single discipline and in the area.

Many more data about the availability of interdisciplinary degree and certificate programs at the NDEA centers are given in Table 7 (page 86). It should be noted that in compiling the statistics for Table 7, we have not counted the third program type described in the list given above. Under that plan, the degree is awarded by a department in a single discipline, but the student works under the guidance of a special interdepartmental committee. Such a plan operates, for example, in the case of doctoral candidates working in the

South Asia Language and Area Center at the University of Chicago. The degree is actually awarded by a department in a particular discipline which controls, as a general rule, about two-thirds of the student's work for the doctorate.

Our data show further that almost 600 graduate students taking work in the NDEA centers in the fall semester 1960 were being helped by a scholarship or fellowship awarded them specifically to do graduate work in language and area studies. Of these graduate students, well over a third are working in the Slavic and East European area, and about a third are working in one of the areas of East and South Asia. For the remaining world areas the percentages are: Middle Eastern, about 10 percent; African, about 7 percent; Luso-Brazilian, about 5 percent. Detailed figures for each world area and for various types of fellowship aid are given in Table 16 (page 93).

CENTER PROGRAMS FOR UNDERGRADUATE STUDENTS

The inventory data show that 469 undergraduates were studying for their B.A. degree with majors or minors in language or area (or both language and area) at the NDEA centers during the fall semester 1960. Of these, over half were at East Asian centers and over a fourth were at Slavic and East European centers. Table 15 gives additional data.

At thirty of the centers (or 65 percent), interdisciplinary B.A. programs are available. Three of the centers have such a program available as a minor or certificate program only, but the remainder have major interdisciplinary programs available to their undergraduates. Table 7 gives additional data on these degree programs.

It is clear from the inventory data, however, that most of the undergraduates in the centers except those in the Slavic programs are studying area rather than language courses. *When this fact was pointed out at the conferences, the representatives agreed that students at the centers should begin language study much earlier than they now do.*

At the conference for representatives from the Middle Eastern centers, this problem was discussed in some detail. The representative from Harvard University stated that if all courses at the Harvard center are considered, there is a somewhat larger number of undergraduates than graduates. But in the language courses, the graduates are vastly in the majority. During the same discussion, the representative from the University of Michigan pointed out that the language staff in the center there have designed their courses at a level of learning and performance expected of graduates.

One of the center directors told our visitor that the dearth of undergraduates is "especially frustrating." He asked that steps be taken to persuade students "of the importance of the rarely taught languages, so that undergraduates would get started in them early in their college careers." At three of the conferences, *center representatives recommended that incentive scholarships be established for undergraduates to encourage study in the critical languages.*

Center representatives at Conference I discussed at some length the public relations and information activities necessary to increase undergraduate enrollments at the centers. The question was asked whether these were tasks which the staffs of NDEA language and area centers should undertake. Conference members pointed out that with limited manpower resources, "time is indeed the most valuable commodity we possess," and choices therefore have to be made of where and how it should be spent. In general, it was assumed that experts in language and area should not spend their time performing special "public relations" tasks. But the discussion nevertheless made it clear that no provision had as yet been made for others to do them.

Special area courses have been designed for undergraduates at a number of the centers. These are described in the section on "Area Studies: Course Offerings," pages 30–31.

ELEMENTS CONTRIBUTING TO CENTER UNITY

It would be logical to assume that the feeling of unity among center staff is directly related to the way a center is organized and administered. If language and area offerings are given within a single administrative unit on a campus, planned by a single director to whom both language and area staff are responsible, it is obvious that the center will be more unified than where this is not the case—if all other factors are equal.

But our visitors found that many other factors—elements outside the formal structure of a center—assumed an important role in establishing and maintaining a sense of unity at a center. The most common device reported in our inventories is the periodic luncheon or meeting arranged by the center for language and area staff. Whenever these took place during periods when our project visitors were at a center, they were, of course, invited to them. Some of these meetings left a deep impression, according to inventory reports.

This meeting is a wholesome affair, strongly unifying people from far-apart fields.

Weekly luncheon meetings provide the occasion for frequent interdepartmental contacts. The project visitor sampled these and was impressed by the spirit of cooperation and the stimulus provided at these occasions.

There are no weekly lunches, no meetings, no formal arrangements of any sort; personal discussions are the only "practices" contributing to center unity.

Other unifying elements which our visitors reported as particularly effective included: the full-time bibliographer who is in contact with all of the faculty working in a given area; physical proximity, with center personnel housed on the same floor or in the same suite of offices; a research program in which many center personnel participate either officially or unofficially; an extracurriculum for students in which center faculty are also intimately involved.

Our visits persuaded us, however, that in the last analysis, the most significant factors contributing to center unity cannot be quantified, and cannot perhaps even be observed directly. One of our visitors, for example, reported: "The strongest contributory factor to center unity here is one most elusive for inventory purposes; it is the personal and professional commitment of the people in the program."

Instruction in Area Studies

The National Defense Education Act of 1958 specifies that in addition to the study of modern foreign languages which are considered critical and for which adequate instruction is not available, the centers may give instruction "in other fields needed to provide a full understanding of the areas, regions, or countries in which such language is commonly used . . . , including fields such as history, political science, linguistics, economics, sociology, geography, and anthropology." (Public Law 85-864, section 601a.)

At several of the conferences, however, some representatives of the centers were not fully satisfied with this relatively simple definition of the term "area studies." For example, at Conference III, when some of the members asserted that the term refers mainly to course offerings in the various social sciences, including history, this statement did not prove generally acceptable. In defending it, one of the speakers said that "when one speaks of people in African 'area studies,' he does not include the man who goes to Africa to study snakes." But another conferee pointed out that certain of the natural sciences, like microbiology and parasitology, were in fact important in African studies. Toward the close of the discussion, there was general agreement that the term could actually refer to every study except the study of the foreign language itself, and that it mainly involved the other humanities (such as art, music, and literature), and all of the social sciences, including history.

Yet, one of the conference members remained dissatisfied. He said this rather simple definition "was certainly adequate for all practical purposes," but asserted that the conference would surely not wish to rest content with it. He went on to make two points. First, the definition avoids completely the precise place and role of linguistics. Second, there are ways in which the study of a language itself serves an "area" rather than a "language" purpose. For example, a diplomat is assigned to an area where language X is spoken, but his official duties do not require him to use language X. Still, he can do his assigned job better if he understands more fully the values, the mental universe, the attitudes toward self and group, and the like, dominant among the speakers of language X. If a study of the language itself will give this diplomat these kinds of insights, then his purpose in studying the language is identical with that served by area studies, since the end of the language study, in this case, is not the actual use of the language but a fuller "understanding of the areas, regions, or countries in which such language is commonly used."

The relationship and distinction between language study and area studies, therefore, appeared not to be as clean-cut as is commonly assumed.

AREA STUDIES PROGRAM: RAISON D'ETRE

Whatever definition one might choose for the term "area studies," our data make it quite clear that there has been extensive encouragement and support for area studies programs at the institutions where

NDEA centers are located. We feel it important to describe the bases for such support, as they have emerged from our analysis of the data collected through center visits and conferences.

This analysis shows that among the administrators and faculty members now supporting area studies programs, two major—and opposed—attitudes are dominant. One view holds that such programs are a positive good, and expresses the hope that American higher education will be permanently affected by them. The other holds that they are basically an educational evil, but at the present time a necessary one, and expresses the hope that as the non-Western civilizations arrive at their proper place in American college and university curricula, area programs will ultimately be eliminated altogether. This opposition was clear not only during our visits to various centers, but it emerged with extraordinary sharpness at the five conferences.

A number (but not an overwhelming number) of center administrative officers and faculty hold the first view. They look upon the development of area studies as a force for good, and they hope that area studies programs will grow and flourish not only for the non-Western areas and cultures, but for Western areas and cultures as well, where such programs are now much less common.

These center personnel frankly believe that American higher education has become excessively fragmented, that doctoral programs have become unnecessarily narrow, and that the humanistic and social science disciplines (not to mention the natural sciences) are tending to develop in isolation on many of the larger campuses; they claim, indeed, that staff members are losing (and want to continue to lose) their sense of interrelationship with other fields of scholarship.

They do not, we discovered, necessarily feel that the division of knowledge by disciplines is in itself an evil, but they assert that it fosters a tendency toward intellectual isolation which can be corrected only through applying certain balances. They claim that integrated programs organized by world area (or in other feasible, interdisciplinary ways) can provide one of these balances. They insist that the area framework constitutes an equally valuable way of extending knowledge through research and transmitting it through teaching.

Adherents of this view therefore welcome the growth of area programs in the non-Western civilizations, foster and participate in such programs whenever possible, and, in addition, encourage colleagues on their campuses who are engaged in such programs in Western areas, such as American Studies or Latin-American Studies. They hope to see a crisscrossing of research and teaching units develop at American universities, with the area representing one axis and the discipline the other axis, each with equal status and prestige.

Our data show that the overwhelming majority of NDEA center administrative and teaching personnel do not accept this view.

They hold that the traditional disciplines ought to continue to be the primary units of research and teaching in American higher education. They have encouraged the growth of area studies because they have felt the non-Western areas must be "covered" somehow in the curriculum, but they would like to see area programs gradually reduced (and finally eliminated), as the study of non-Western areas moves toward the stage of development and prestige on American campuses that Western Europe now enjoys. They point out that no such program as Western European Area Studies exists. They insist that such a program would be patently superfluous, since Western Europe is well "covered" by every discipline in the humanities and the social sciences at practically every university. They hope eventually to see the current area programs also become superfluous.

NDEA language and area centers cannot refuse to participate in this basic controversy, since a view on this question must be taken by the instructional or administrative officers who are responsible for making decisions about the center's formal structure.

At Conference I, one of the representatives from the University of Pennsylvania pointed out that every campus has tried to solve this problem, but it is essentially insoluble. All resolutions are "somewhat uncomfortable" in the last analysis. This speaker went on to say that the center of gravity must be placed either in area or in the discipline, and in either case there are tremendous disadvantages.

Several conferees argued that decisions of this sort must be based on an educational philosophy rather than on expediency or on the current fashion in the academic world. At Conference II, the intensity of the discussion on this question can be judged by one sentence, taken from the conference report: "One of the conferees then asked: 'Isn't the notion of "area study" an enormous illusion?' "

At Conference III, several representatives pointed to the greater "marketability" of a traditional degree in a discipline. One conference member argued that it is, indeed, desirable to integrate various disciplines as they bear on a given problem; but this attempt should be made only after one has mastered a single discipline. Moreover, it was argued, scholarly activity of that sort might well be delayed until one has become an established scholar and is secure in his position. The best advice to the graduate student is, therefore, to follow strictly the line set down by a particular scholarly discipline.

This argument was opposed by other conference members on three grounds. First, for students who will eventually seek career opportunities outside the academic world, the broader training may well be more appropriate than the narrower, departmental training. Second, even within the academic world, in graduate schools, this basic issue of educational philosophy is not settled. Third, not every Ph.D. wishes to spend his life in an academic institution primarily geared to the production of Ph.D.'s. Many would prefer to move to an undergraduate college, where the applicant with the broader and more integrated background would make the more effective teacher for undergraduates.

At Conference V, the discussion yielded an illustration of the kinds of "real problems in society" which, it was claimed, cannot be adequately analyzed if they are approached from the compartmentalized points of view represented by the various academic disciplines. An example was given at the conference:

If one were analyzing the problem of the population explosion in Asia, conference members were asked, which discipline would be appropriate? The problem can be approached by the sociologist, but before his analysis moves very far, the economist must be asked to step forward in order to analyze the relevant economic factors. The two together, however, cannot present an acceptable analysis of the whole unless colleagues from other disciplines join them in analyzing certain moral and religious elements as well as certain biological and medical factors which would also play major roles in any decision about the most effective course of future action.

This example, it was claimed, shows that real problems (as opposed to academic problems) can be adequately analyzed only from a multidisciplinary point of view.

Nevertheless, in the conference discussions, as in our center visits, we found a strong tendency on the part of the majority of center personnel to regard as primary the organization of the fields of knowledge in terms of disciplines, and to look upon all other modes of organizing knowledge and scholarship as capable of playing only a secondary or occasional role. The division of the fields of scholarship by discipline, they seem to think, is the logical, natural division.

This view appears to us to be questionable, on the level of both fact and theory. Aside from one's discipline, there appear to us to be at least three different ways in which scholars in the social sciences and the humanities, when they talk about their "fields," may identify their research and study. Indeed, an identifying statement will often classify a man's field simultaneously in two or three—or perhaps all four—of the following categories:

1. His *discipline:* the name which describes the set of methods and tools that the scholar uses—political science; philosophy; history; etc.

2. The *object* of his research: its substantive rather than its methodological aspect—the elementary school; village organization; surrealism; nationalism; etc.

3. His *area:* the site of his research—the United States; Western Europe; the Far East; sub-Saharan Africa; the Mediterranean Basin; etc.

4. The *epoch:* the temporal context of the object of research: the ancient world; the Renaissance; the Age of Reason—to name only a few of the common period designations in Western civilization.

Sometimes the relations among these four aspects of a field are somewhat complex. The discipline of one field may be the object of investigation in another; thus, the *method of the sciences* may be a research *object* for a philosopher; or *research in the classical field* during the second half of the nineteenth century in the United States may be a research *object* for a man in American studies. But normally these relationships are brought out when we name a field: German romanticism; modern European history; the Soviet economy.

If a scholar habitually identifies himself as an anthropologist, the likelihood is that his *discipline* organizes his thought and study. But a second scholar may habitually identify his field as the theater, and we assume that, for him, the *object* of his research, substantively, is more significant than his discipline; indeed, he may be trained in more than one. A third says he is an Africanist; for him the *area* of research constitutes the crux. And a fourth tells us he is a medievalist. For him the *epoch* marks his field of study, and we do not know from the label alone whether the object of his research is a kingdom, a cathedral, a world view, a page of illuminated manuscript, or some interrelationship among these.

Each axis described above, and perhaps some others as well, appears to us to constitute a legitimate organizing principle for a field of scholarship. We do not see how any one of the four can be put forward as the single key to the organization of scholarship and knowledge.

Above all, viewed functionally, in his daily and hourly activities on the campus, a scholar cannot be identified by one of the categories only. During one hour his field is the Enlightenment; in another context, he is a French scholar; in a third, he is a drama man; on another day, he may be a literary critic. In a fifth context, he is not eighteenth-century, nor literary, nor French—for, in discussing certain problems central to his own field but which the several arts find in common, he is a humanities man. These are *all* his field, variously defined according to different contexts.

To which department shall he then be assigned? This is a crucial question, for on many campuses his departmental assignment determines many details of daily life. His department is where he is assigned an office, receives his mail, seeks secretarial help, and finds his closest professional associates. His department is where his promotion and tenure are decided. These, surely, are not matters that can be tucked under the blotter. And above all—since departments exist also for students—here is where students' academic lives will be formed and guided.

We believe the American administrative mind is ingenious enough to conceive a plan whereby academic departments can be organized to carry out the administrative details of college life efficiently, without fixing forever in some single mold—as if decreed by nature—the organization of knowledge.

AREA STUDIES: COURSE OFFERINGS

As we noted earlier, over 1,200 courses were offered in language and area at the forty-six centers during the autumn semester 1960. Of these a little over half (53 percent) were in area studies. Of the almost 650 area courses offered in the centers, about thirty were listed in the field of linguistics. If one does not count the courses in linguistics, proportions among the various fields ran as follows:

Departmental courses in the social sciences 36%
Departmental courses in the humanities 25%
Departmental courses in history 23%
Interdepartmental courses 16%

Additional data on these categories and a further breakdown into particular disciplines are given in Table 14 (page 91).

The individual inventory reports contain detailed descriptions of many of the interdepartmental courses. Our data show about a hundred of these courses in existence at the centers at the time our survey was made. Many of these are designed for undergraduates and constitute part of the general education programs on various campuses.

At the conference for NDEA representatives from East Asian language and area centers, for example, the representative from the University of Michigan described a course on Asia which is designed to satisfy the distribution requirement for undergraduates in either social science or humanities. The representative from Columbia described two courses in the general education program—one of them entitled "Oriental Civilizations" and the other a course in the Oriental humanities. The latter course is given in the form of a colloquium and is organized by a list of major works which the students read and come to class to discuss.

The inventory reports show that in the development of such courses, the centers have been influenced by one another. The report from the South Asia Center at the University of Wisconsin, for example, describes the introduction of the interdepartmental, undergraduate course in the civilization of India as a "significant step." It was modeled on the course given at the University of Chicago South Asia Center, and was evolved at Wisconsin from existing resources, without additional funds of any sort. Similarly, when the Center for Middle Eastern Studies at Harvard University started its program, there was no general course on the Middle East. Such a course on the Far East—known as "Rice Paddies"—had been given, our visitor reported, with great success for more than ten years. A Middle East course was accordingly devised, combining contributions from anthropology, economics, history, and other departments, and was accepted for Harvard's general education program. It is known as "Flying Carpet."

While some of these courses have a long history and their staff has much experience, our visitors discovered at a number of centers that such courses were being given for the first time in the autumn of 1960. At the University of Hawaii, for example, an integrated area course entitled "Civilizations of the East" was organized during that semester and being given for the first time. While the chairman of the history department serves as course chairman, staff members for the course are being drawn from more than ten departments.

It would be inaccurate to give the impression that courses of an interdisciplinary nature are designed for undergraduates only, as part of the general education programs. Our reports indicate that a number of centers have interdepartmental seminars for graduate students. At Michigan, there is an integrated course on the graduate level devoted to the scope and methods of research on the Near East. At the Southeast Asia Language and Area Center at Cornell University, there is a "country" seminar—a graduate seminar dealing with a different country each term. In 1959–60 it dealt with Burma, and in the fall of 1960–61, with Malaya. It is always a multiple-instructor course.

As a general rule, our visitors reported that they found the interdepartmental area courses more imaginatively conceived, more carefully planned, and more excitingly taught than the more traditional departmental courses.

The Role of Linguistics at the NDEA Centers

Linguistics is a young discipline in the American academic world, and its administrative location on most campuses is both puzzling and unsatisfactory. It is often placed within the anthropology department, since it is one of the major tools of the cultural anthropologist. Sometimes it is a separate department. When it does have this status, we found its nature and structure very different as we moved from one campus to the next. One of our visitors wrote about one such department, "The Linguistics Department has been, and still is, to some extent a shelter for homeless languages." Another visitor reported that two NDEA centers which he had visited were located in the linguistics department because there did not appear to be any other department in which to house the languages and staff which constitute the language side of those centers.

In many ways, linguistics plays an important role at the NDEA centers. But not many of the centers maintain a formal relationship with the linguistics department on their campus. Illustrative are comments from the inventory reports: "There are at present no formal relations with the Department of Linguistics." "Since Professor F. left, center ties with the Department of Linguistics no longer exist." "There is no close tie-in with the offerings in linguistics." "Linguistics, as such, does not play a vital role in center course offerings."

Insofar as the wording of title VI goes, linguistics simply appears as one of the disciplines "needed to provide a full understanding of the areas, regions, or countries" where a given foreign language is used. Hence, it finds itself in the same category as geography, political science, anthropology, philosophy, or history. It is obvious, of course, that the field of linguistics does not fall into the category "area studies," nor yet is work in linguistics the same as the study of a language. It seemed to come closest to area studies at the African centers, but, even there, a course in phonetics and phonemics with special reference to certain sub-Saharan languages, for example, would hardly be fulfilling purposes of the sort set for area courses in African geography, for example, or the peoples of Africa. Nor does such a linguistics course fulfill the same purposes as a course (such as Swahili or Twi) in a specific language. The role of linguistics in the centers has been distinct, and we believe it should be analyzed apart from the work in language and area studies.

Linguistics has played an important role at some of the NDEA centers on both the theoretical level (or, as it is sometimes stated, in its "pure" form) and on the applied level. In its so-called pure form, work in linguistics sometimes precedes the study of a specific language or accompanies such study, as a means of facilitating and quickening the process of language mastery; or, in the case of prospective language teachers, it may not appear in their programs until their professional training as future teachers begins.

At Conference III, one of the speakers was emphatic about the benefits which would accrue if special courses were designed "in descriptive linguistics for students of foreign languages." This speaker said that he would prefer students to have had a course in descriptive linguistics before they begin the study of a particular foreign language. There was, however, disagreement on this point, several conference members stoutly maintaining that they would accept this requirement only for students of a foreign language who intended to teach that language.

On that particular point, however, there was consensus at the conferences. At Conferences III and IV, for example, it was agreed that (*a*) language teachers ought to have training in linguistics, and (*b*) by and large the people who are engaged in the teaching of language at the present time do not have sufficient training in linguistics, especially of the descriptive variety. At Conference IV, however, there were a few conferees who openly regarded the value of linguistics as undemonstrated. One of the representatives said: "The linguist has come upon the scene rather recently, and I would like to give him a little more time to prove his value before I could recommend that we require our students to take his courses."

At Conference V, the representative from the University of Michigan outlined the requirements in descriptive linguistics for all center students going into the teaching field. Our inventory data indicate, however, that required course work in descriptive linguistics for future teachers of language is the exception rather than the rule at NDEA centers.

Center faculty members, it goes without saying, could not be expected to support such a requirement unless they themselves had had some training in descriptive linguistics. In some centers, our visitors' reports show, this is clearly the case. For example, one of our reports reads: "All of the language faculty at this center seem to have been much influenced by contemporary thinking in American linguistics." The report then describes the way in which the language courses are organized, the selection of textbooks, the role of the language laboratory, and the actual methods used in the classroom; and all of these substantiate the generalization made by our visitor. At another center, on the other hand, just the opposite condition is described: "None of the faculty seem to have been influenced in their structural analyses or their teaching method by the concepts developed in this country in the field of descriptive linguistics during the past quarter century."

The application of the principles of descriptive linguistics to the teaching of foreign languages is itself a controversial subject in modern language circles. The assertion, therefore, that a center's faculty have, or have not, been influenced by the principles of linguistics is to be read as a purely descriptive statement. In our inventory reports, neither comment is intended to be taken as either favorable or unfavorable.

No such neutrality was maintained, however, by center representatives when this issue was discussed at conferences. Several of the conferences praised the contribution of both theoretical and applied linguists to second language pedagogics. At Conference V, in particular, it was pointed out that the work of the linguists has proved extremely helpful to the teacher of languages, and that the experiments which are being carried on in applied linguistics can "teach language teachers a great deal about practices, techniques, and devices that would serve to make language teaching more efficient."

Since relations have sometimes not been cordial between linguists and language teachers, this specific subject was brought up and discussed frankly at Conference V. One of the speakers stated that misunderstandings often arise because linguists, and sometimes the language teachers, too, are unwilling to explain a point with sufficient patience. Further, it was pointed out that all too often both sides become so defensive about their point of view that intelligent communication is impossible.

Even though our inventory shows that comparatively little work is now being pursued by center students in descriptive linguistics (other than the work which they would normally do as part of their study of a specific language), *there was very clear agreement at Conferences IV and V about the value of the study of descriptive linguistics for the prospective teacher of languages.*

The Teaching of the Critical Languages

We have already mentioned that the forty-six NDEA centers gave 550 courses in over forty languages to about 7,000 students during the fall semester 1960. Over 3,000 of these students were enrolled in first-year language courses. About 300 staff members holding academic rank taught the center language courses, and about 200 more served as instructional assistants: informants, drill masters, teaching assistants, and laboratory technicians.

COMMITMENT TO THE AUDIO-LINGUAL APPROACH

Since the end of the Second World War, college teachers of foreign languages have become more and more aware of the principles governing the audio-lingual approach to language teaching.[2] Our inventory shows that many of the older language and area centers were influenced by these new methods during their pre-NDEA life. Indeed, several of the universities on the centers list—Cornell, Michigan, Yale, to name only three—have assumed leadership, during the last quarter century, in formulating the theoretical bases upon which an audio-lingual approach to the teaching of a second language may be built. In addition, a large number of the NDEA centers are located at universities that have been working out ways of implementing these principles. In observing these attempts at implementation, we noticed that the plans devised at such institutions as Cornell and Yale played an important role. For example, our visitor to one center stated in his inventory report that he was told, "We are attempting to follow the Cornell plan." Another of our visitors, reporting from another center, stated, "Instructors are asked to conform as closely as possible to the Yale system."

On the whole, those centers which committed themselves to the audio-lingual approach during the years of their foreign area and language programs under the ASTP have remained committed to it. For example, our visitor at one center reported that during the Second World War, at the time the university had ASTP units, present center personnel were "exposed to the 'newer language teaching methods'" to which they were "soon converted as they gained experience." Our visitor quotes the comment of one of the key language staff members at the center: "We were never the same again."

But the majority of the 1960–61 NDEA centers cannot be said to have committed themselves fully to the audio-lingual approach. The inventory data indicate that twelve centers—a fourth of the total number—are fully committed. At these centers, the audio-lingual approach is dominant not only in principle but also in center practice.

[2] An exposition of these principles is presented in Appendix A.

At eleven additional centers, our data indicate that on the theoretical level the program is largely, though not fully, committed to this approach. At the centers in this second category, the project visitors observed many audio-lingual features in classroom practice. They even described some classes in their reports which read like model examples of this method. Yet, in analyzing the whole language program at the center, we have concluded that this method is not dominant in daily practice.

At half of the centers, then, the language program is either fully or largely committed in principle to the audio-lingual approach. Complete data with respect to this commitment may be found in Table 11 (page 89). Attention should be called to the fact, for it is relevant to the interpretation of these data, that in administering the NDEA center program, the Office of Education has taken no official position on the teaching methods to be used in center language training.

ATTITUDE TOWARD LANGUAGE AS A WORTHY TEACHING AND RESEARCH SUBJECT

For language teachers on the college and university level, commitment to the audio-lingual approach is closely bound to an interest in linguistic analysis and in problems of teaching a second language effectively. It is, therefore, not surprising to find that, as a general rule, those centers which are fully or largely committed to the audio-lingual approach look upon a foreign language as a worthy teaching subject for the college professor, and they regard the analysis of linguistic forms and structures (and the problems of teaching them to students whose first language is English) as a respectable field for scholarly research.

In the past, on a very large number of American campuses, a faculty member's work in foreign languages was commonly regarded —by himself and by his colleagues—as merely an adjunct to some other, more respectable, scholarly or pedagogical goal. Usually this was the study and teaching of the foreign literature. This attitude is still, of course, commonly encountered, but our inventory contains ample evidence to suggest that at the majority of the NDEA centers, it is at present not the dominant attitude.

Our visitor at the East Asian Language and Area Center at Columbia University, for example, reported that during his visits, the center language staff was in the midst of discussions of a basic policy document which was then still in draft form. Two sections of that document are entitled "Departmental Policies in Regard to Language Teachers" and "Principles Governing Language Instruction." One of the policies set forth in the first-named section specifies that research in teaching methods and the improvement of teaching materials should serve as one basis for advancement in academic rank, in precisely the way the more usual forms of scholarly publication are considered when a faculty member comes up for promotion.

The section on the principles governing language instruction makes clear that the audio-lingual approach is generally to be adopted. It also specifies that the reading ability is at all times to remain a major goal and is to be given increased emphasis in the third-year course and in more advanced courses. In this connection, the document suggests that beyond the second-year course, separate advanced courses should be made available to develop more highly the students' speaking skill. As the analysis in Appendix A makes clear, there is no inconsistency between the audio-lingual approach on the college level and the adoption of reading skill as a primary goal.

There is other evidence which shows that, at the centers, structural analysis of a foreign language and the creation of new teaching materials are considered worthy study and research pursuits for the college professor of language. Perhaps the clearest single piece of evidence lies in the fact that so many of the language personnel at the NDEA centers are engaged, in addition to their teaching, in precisely this kind of research and writing. Our data show that this is the case in almost exactly 60 percent of the centers. Much of this research is of course stimulated, or actually supported, by NDEA research funds under title VI. Undoubtedly the availability of these funds has helped to widen the circle marking the kinds of scholarly activities that are considered respectable by the college teaching profession at large.

Whatever the cause, it seems clear that this circle has been widened in many academic communities, for it now includes work in analyzing contrastive structures in English and many foreign languages, preparing courses of study, writing graded readers, constructing laboratory drills and recording them on tapes, and experimenting in teaching methodology.

At a number of the centers, this new research and the actual teaching of language have, indeed, become interdependent. Our individual inventories contain observations such as these: "Since most of the staff is working on teaching materials for publication, the classroom becomes the laboratory for the teacher, who learns by teaching and who tests the materials in class." Again: "The NDEA research contract is one of the pillars of language instruction here. The teaching materials which are prepared under this project are tested in the classes held in the center and, in turn, receive stimuli from these classes."

When a center looks upon problems in applied linguistics and in language teaching methodology as subjects that ought to be *beneath* the college professor's central research interests, our analysis shows that this attitude is reflected in (*a*) the plans which the center graduate students make for their own future, and in (*b*) the M.A. and Ph.D. programs that those students are asked to pursue at the center. One example of each, taken from our reports, will suffice as illustrations.

At one such center (where the director expressed hostility to the audio-lingual approach), our visitor interviewed an unusually promising graduate student who currently holds a fellowship and plans to become a college language teacher. Part of the report of this interview runs as follows: "Mr. S. is very much interested in linguistics. But problems of teaching courses in language, he said, frankly do not sustain his interest. He is attracted to 'more scholarly' pursuits."

At a second institution, all of the graduate courses in language at the center (except for a proseminar in research tools) consist in the reading of belletristic texts and other literary documents such as historical works, philosophic treatises, and the like. No course in the graduate program is designed primarily to increase the M.A. or Ph.D. candidate's linguistic skills. No graduate course is primarily concerned with such aspects of the language as its phonemics or morphology.

Our visitor, in reporting this fact, also added the personal note that, in his experience with graduate curricula in the European languages, he found precisely this curricular pattern obtaining whenever the attitude pervasive in a language department saw the teaching of languages as a tedious and demeaning but unavoidable activity in the academic life of the instructor or young professor of language and literature.

On the whole, our data clearly show that this attitude is not dominant at the NDEA language and area centers. Indeed, at the majority of the centers encouragement is now being given to center language staff members, through promotion in rank and through increased status among colleagues, to construct new teaching materials, to collect new data about instructional method, and to engage in a whole range of other research and writing projects in the fields of applied linguistics and pedagogics.

COLLEGE AND UNIVERSITY GOALS SERVED
BY THE CENTER LANGUAGE COURSES

The first of the conferences called for representatives of the NDEA centers posed the question of what the language training aims of an NDEA center ought to be. "It became clear," the report of that conference states, that these "could not really be stated in any precise terms"; it could only be said that "the central aim was to give a useful command of the language." This statement of aim was intended to include (a) the person who would have to deal with government officials, for whom a spoken knowledge of the language would be useful, as well as (b) the person who works only with printed materials. The definition also, of course, includes every situation which one might find in between the two given in these examples.

The subsequent conferences as well as the center visits themselves made clear the three sharply different main goals which are now being served by the language courses given at the NDEA centers:

1. The study of a language for its broadening and liberating effects and, in particular, for the insights such study can give into the structure of the emotional world and the modes of thought within which speakers of that language live;
2. The acquisition of the language as a professional tool, for example, for the political scientist who must be able to read newspapers in the foreign language in order to make his analyses, for the anthropologist who is preparing to live in a village where the foreign language only is spoken, and so on;
3. The advanced program in language for the future teacher and/or scholar in language and literature.

The first two functions are sometimes referred to as service functions. Language courses which fulfill the first function contribute to the general education (or liberal arts) goals of the college or university of which the NDEA center is a part. Language courses fulfilling the second function contribute to the program designed for students in the area departments. Only in the case of the third function are the time and energy of the language staff expended on behalf of the student actually majoring in language.

Exactly how a center should proportion its funds and its human and material resources among these three main functions appears to be a problem about which there is some disagreement among center personnel. For example, at Conference II, the discussion tried to sharpen the issues revolving around the purposes of language training at a university—especially the nonscholarly, or service, functions —and to resolve the dilemma of how much time and energy the departmental staff should devote to each of the different functions.

Some conference members opposed the distinction between the scholarly and the service functions of language departments and argued that every course which teaches a skill that is not a goal in itself (for example, courses in bibliography or in methods of research) is a service course.

Some conference members seemed particularly disturbed at the suggestion that the primary function of a language department was to perform services for other parts of the university program. Although this opinion was not held by any of the conferees, some campus administrators expressed precisely this view to our visitors during the center visits. One of our reports, for example, reads: "The dean of the Social Science Division posed the question whether the language side of the center will ever be more than a service to the area side." Or again: "Growth of population, according to the director, seems tied in with growth in the area program. Without some local field applicability of the languages to area subjects, there is little hope for an increase in language class enrollments."

In the critical languages which are no longer uncommon on American campuses, the problem is more general, but it nevertheless persists. One of our visitors reported: "In a sense, the language is so definitely a tool—an accessory of sorts—for center students, that a serious problem exists for the Slavic Department."

As the next section, describing the patterns of course organization in language departments, will show, those language departments that have the most efficient organization appear to be the ones which have made an analysis of the precise goals which their language courses are to serve; and they have then planned their course offerings on the basis of this analysis. In some cases, as will be seen, this plan calls for different courses offered at the same language level but designed for different goals.

PATTERNS OF COURSE ORGANIZATION
AND CLASSROOM INSTRUCTION

Most first- and second-year language courses given on American campuses have been multipurpose in their aims; and the organization of the courses has reflected this attempt on the part of college language teachers to meet different goals through the same course or course sequence. But since the various functions served by first- and second-year language courses in academic institutions are so very different, it is considered desirable by many language teachers to have more than one sequence of courses in the foreign language starting on the elementary level, each specifically designed for a given goal. Certainly, the kind of elementary language course which would best serve a general education goal would be differently designed from the kind of language course which would best serve a research tool goal.

This differentiation between the general education function of a language course for the undergraduate and the research tool function for the graduate is especially germane in the case of the graduate student who must be given a useful command of the foreign language quickly. In most area programs, graduate students will not be permitted to go very far in their studies without at least a reading knowledge of one of the leading languages of the area. At the conferences called for representatives of the centers, there was general agreement that the tool function of language study cannot be effectively fulfilled unless the student has had a minimum of three college years of work in the language as an undergraduate or study in graduate school giving equivalent mastery.

All of the graduate NDEA centers have been aware of this problem. A large number of them have in fact designed special first- and second-year language courses for the graduate student primarily, by which they hope the research tool function will be fulfilled more effectively than through the usual undergraduate language courses. These are intensive language courses with eight or more contact hours weekly. Two-thirds of the graduate centers offer such courses. They were given at 50 percent of the centers in the autumn semester 1960. Of the 50 percent which did not give them, just under 10 percent are undergraduate centers, and just over 10 percent had given such courses during the preceding summer. The remaining 30 percent are graduate centers, then, which did not give such courses either in the summer or fall of 1960. At all except one of the centers at which they were given in the autumn semester, these intensive courses were "double courses" meeting eight, nine, or ten hours each week. At many centers, there are six-contact-hour language courses, often called "semi-intensive"; but courses with fewer than eight contact hours per week were not counted in the category for which figures are being given here. Additional data on this point may be found in Table 10 (page 88).

At many of the centers giving intensive courses with eight or more contact hours per week, such courses are not open to undergraduates. At other centers, undergraduates are eligible to take such courses, but typically they do not do so. For example, at the Center for Middle Eastern Studies at Harvard University, a non-intensive course in contemporary Arabic is not offered. Undergraduates who wish to study Arabic, therefore, either begin with the course in classical Arabic (which is not formally related to the NDEA center) or they may take the intensive course in the contemporary language, designed primarily for graduates. But in all the language courses given at that center, our data show, the graduates are in the vast majority. The same situation was reported for the language courses at the Center for East Asian Studies at Harvard, but that center is now planning, after a lapse of a decade, to resume non-intensive courses.

At the East Asian Center at Columbia University, both types of courses are given. The course designed primarily for graduates meets ten hours per week, with two additional hours in the language laboratory and a thirty-minute weekly session in the language clinic. The majority of students in the course have been graduates, only about one-fifth having been undergraduates. The course designed primarily for undergraduates moves at about half the pace, with five hours per week in class and an hour in the laboratory. The Far Eastern Center at the University of Michigan and the Center for Middle Eastern Studies at Princeton have adopted similar solutions.

At one of the centers, our visitor reported that the mixture of undergraduate students (the large majority of whom are taking elementary language work primarily for general education or liberal arts goals) and graduate students (who are taking elementary language primarily as a tool) was abandoned: "It proved to be deleterious to mix the two groups in the same language class, as they are so differently motivated and come with such different training."

The question was raised at several of the conferences whether graduate credit should be given for elementary language courses. A blanket answer was not easy to reach. No one, for example, expected a Russian major to study Serbo-Croatian—even on an elementary level—as an undergraduate; yet it would be unjust to require such study in the student's graduate program and withhold the reward normally given for graduate study.

The ultimate difficulty, it was agreed, lies in the practice of awarding a graduate degree on the basis of credit hours. Degrees, some conferees insisted, should be given on the basis of levels of attainment toward specific goals. There are institutions, it was pointed out, where graduate students do not count up credit hours. They simply enroll in the courses which they need to help them achieve the desired mastery. The degree of achievement is subsequently judged by the instructional staff on the basis of actual performance rather than on the number of credit hours accumulated.

There was agreement at two of the conferences that if a student entering graduate school and planning to do his work in one of the area programs has had no work in language, it would be wise for him to take a "total immersion" program in the language. Most of the centers, especially those which depend for their language training on the double courses during the regular academic year, do not have courses in language so intensive that the student studies nothing else. But approximately a fifth of the centers did offer such courses during the summer session 1960, and one center gave such a course during 1960–61. In this way, the student completes three years of language work in a single academic year or in two full summer sessions (with total immersion in language) and a non-intensive course during the academic year between the two summers.

In two areas—Southeast Asian studies and Middle Eastern studies—interuniversity summer sessions have been successfully instituted. The fifth summer session under the Interuniversity Plan for Middle Eastern Studies was scheduled at Princeton University for the summer of 1961. This program began with five cooperating universities, and now others are joining the plan. The program planned for the summer of 1961 contained offerings in Arabic, Persian, and Turkish, with eight-week courses, each meeting daily for three hours of class and for two or more hours, in addition, in the laboratory. Since 1953 Yale and Cornell have been alternating in giving summer work in Indonesian, both first- and second-year courses. The enrollment in 1960 was thirty-five.

The single disadvantage of this plan, to which representatives at the conferences pointed, is serious: Different centers pace their language programs differently and cover different materials. As a consequence, the amount of variation on both quantitative and qualitative levels is very great. *To meet the difficult problem of course articulation, the members of Conference IV recommended that course syllabi be worked out by national committees representing the institutions participating in any joint program. If this one disadvantage could be conquered, all other conditions favor joint summer programs.* For students, it is salutary to move to another campus for the summer and meet people from other campuses interested in the same area and languages. For staff, this argument is even more germane. Moreover, where the total number of staff personnel teaching a given language throughout the country is small, while it is perhaps well for them to be dispersed during the academic year, offerings must remain relatively thin on any one campus. The joint summer session provides an opportunity for more advanced offerings and a more solid program.

While enthusiasm was expressed, both during our center visits and at the conferences, for an expansion of the full immersion course in language during summer sessions in individual center programs and at joint summer programs—provided adequate financial support for this expansion can be found—there was not, in every quarter, equal enthusiasm for full immersion courses during the academic year. At Conference V, one of the center directors objected to such courses. Would it not be better, he asked, for a student to go to Japan or to Taiwan if he wished to study Chinese or Japanese, and nothing else, for a given period of time? There, he could have his language work reinforced by the environment. This director asserted strongly that there was no place in a liberal arts college, or even in a graduate school, for the full immersion language course during the academic year. He stated that there exists a discrepancy between the goal of intellectual maturity, which is the basic purpose of a university, and a program that excludes all study for an academic year except work in a language.

For the linguists present at the conferences, this point of view presented something of a dilemma. They, of course, also saw as desirable the reinforcement provided by residence in the area where the language is spoken. But the linguists agreed that for the student who is starting his study of a foreign language, it would not be wise to go to the language area in order to study the language.

Five factors were listed that militate against effective language study abroad for the beginning language student: (a) the excitement of being in a new environment, and with it the low motivation for spending a large percentage of one's day in a classroom; (b) the frustration at not knowing the language well enough upon arrival to use it even in routine situations; (c) the heavy dependence on the use of English in one's social and academic contacts—a habit which would prove difficult to break even after language study has enabled the student to communicate on a simple level in the language; (d) the the lack of proper study facilities, personnel, and equipment for language teaching in most foreign areas; and (e) the many residents of foreign lands who wish to be helpful but also wish to practice their English.

For students beyond the beginning stage, however, the advantages of spending part of the graduate years in the area where the language being studied is spoken are obvious. Indeed, the Chinese-Japanese Center at Stanford University has already established a campus in Tokyo, an American center in India is being contemplated by a group of South Asian NDEA centers, and a center located in the Middle East is being planned by one of the Near and Middle Eastern NDEA centers.

Plans for language and area study abroad, under the auspices of an

American university, and the introduction of intensive language courses at individual centers and at joint programs are features of center thought and action that have been conceived and built with the graduate student in mind. Considerably less attention is paid to the undergraduate's language training at most of the centers, but our data show that he is not entirely neglected. For him, language courses normally provide three, four, or five contact hours per week. At this slower pace—there was general agreement on this point at the conferences—anything under three years of work does not result in usable linguistic skills.

Some of the representatives at Conference III, who also agreed with this general point, nevertheless wished to justify the existence of the three-hour-per-week language course. Students may not be able to use the language after they finish a year of study, it was said, and yet—assuming a well-taught course—they will have learned enough to know how to continue their study of the language if they should find themselves in an area where the language is spoken. There is an enormous difference between the student who has this kind of readiness, even though his actual skills may be low, and the student who has had no training in the language in question whatsoever. At Conference III, experience with African languages provided evidence to substantiate this point.

All the courses in language at the four African centers have only three contact hours per week; one of these centers requires, in addition, a weekly laboratory hour. At all other centers, however, language courses of only three contact hours per week are in the minority. Most non-intensive courses meet four, five, or six hours per week.

At Conference V, the question arose as to whether the intensive courses and the non-intensive courses differed only in their quantitative dimension, or whether there were actual qualitative differences between them. The answers given by center representatives indicated that qualitative differences between them can be observed. Students in an intensive course have a far better sense of continuity and a better over-all picture of the structures of the language. During the discussion, some of the center language staff insisted that quantitative comparisons were made only as a matter of convenience; one cannot think of one course, they said, moving at a certain pace, and of another course moving at half or twice the pace of the first.

In all of the language courses—both the non-intensive courses and the ones which have eight or more contact hours per week—our project visitors frequently observed the practice of differentiating between small-group sessions for oral drill and larger class meetings usually called "grammar" or "lecture" periods. One or more of the language courses at 75 percent of the NDEA centers was organized in this way during the autumn semester 1960. For classes with five contact hours per week, the pattern which our visitors found most common showed three of those hours assigned to oral-practice sessions; course patterns assigning two or four hours weekly for this purpose are also to be found at the centers.

There appear to be several reasons why so many of the centers have separated instruction into analysis and practice sessions. One reason is economy. Very highly trained personnel are needed for the analysis sessions; but less expert personnel (usually native speakers of the language hired as instructional assistants) are taught to lead the drill sessions effectively, and thus funds are saved for other purposes. A second reason is that such separation of instruction seems to result in quicker and longer-lasting learning by the student. It is apparently not sound psychologically, and therefore not effective, in elementary language work to combine drill and analysis in a single session as these processes are very different in purpose, in method, and especially in classroom tempo. Moreover, linguistic analysis, which is normally given in lecture form, can be presented to a very large group, but the drill sessions are effective only with a small group.

A third reason lies in the sense of community it provides among the language staff, working as a team.

These are the factors that explain why the system of organizing one or more of the first- and second-year language classes in this particular way obtains at thirty-four of the forty-six centers.

Our visitors observed that the grammar sessions may have as many as eighty or a hundred students, but according to our data, the drill sessions do not have more than fifteen, and usually the number is ten or fewer. Indeed, at Conference I it was proposed that the ideal drill session size is five to eight students. When there are fewer than five, it was stated, instruction suffers.

These points about class size, made by representatives from the centers themselves, agree with observations made earlier by our visitors. For example, one of the project visitors reported from one center as follows: "In none of the language courses does the population, at present, exceed four. This class size permits much more exposure of the class to the team composed of the instructor and the native-speaking drill master than is possible in the more common language courses." At the same time, our visitor posed the question as to whether a very small group offers the instructor or drill master "enough resonance for audio-lingual drill, such as is found in a section of around eight students."

Policies on the hiring of personnel for the language staff of a center will, of course, be affected by the adoption of the plan under which drill sessions and analysis sessions are differentiated. The analysis sessions are normally given in English and must be instructed by a highly trained teacher. A native speaker of the language who has a degree in letters from a fine university does not, by virtue of those facts alone, constitute a qualified teacher of his language, especially for the sessions in grammatical analysis. At Conference III, this point was particularly emphasized. One of the conferees hit hard at the common assumption that native competence in itself qualifies a person to teach a language.

Under the plan of differentiating analysis sessions from practice sessions, the center engages a number of native speakers of the language who serve as informants during the analysis session. Often, of course, the person analyzing the grammar is himself a native speaker and may therefore function as informant as well as analyst. Occasionally this dual role is unsucccessful, as in the following case, reported by one of our visitors: "The impression gained was that the dual role of informant and linguistically trained instructor is difficult to play. In this particular case, the lack of English, which in itself is desirable in a drill session, is a handicap when it comes to instruction in grammatical analysis."

There appears to be some disagreement among center directors or those in charge of the language program at the center (usually language department chairmen) about the qualifications for the staff members who are to serve as drill masters in the practice sessions and also, if necessary, as informants in the analysis sessions. At one of the centers it is believed that, with respect to drill sessions, "any educated native of lively personality can do the job well if he is adequately trained and supervised." At another center, our visitor reported that "the use of a native speaker who is linguistically 'uneducated' or 'innocent' is not considered good practice."

At those centers which do not differentiate in a systematic way in any of their language courses between grammatical analysis sessions and drill sessions (this covers a fourth of the NDEA centers), the position of drill master or informant simply does not exist. Our visitor reported from one center: "There are no linguistic informants, as such; the director doesn't believe in them." From another center, our visitor reported that the director complained because classes were too large; yet they could not be split into sections, the director claimed, because this "would mean doubling the teaching staff and it is too expensive an operation." After reporting this fact, our visitor added the personal note: "A planned use of native speakers as drill masters could help solve this problem without greatly increased expense. This possibility, however, is apparently not being considered."

At two of the conferences, *the importance of inservice training for the native speakers hired as drill masters or informants was emphasized*. At Conference I, it was pointed out that however desirable such training might be, in many cases the informants do not stay in the program long enough to give time for, or to justify, an orientation program for them. At Conference III, one of the center directors, a linguist who teaches Swahili, told of the case of his informant who was otherwise adequate but constantly raised objection to the linguist's phonemic transcription of Swahili whenever it did not correspond with traditional orthography.

Whether or not a center adopts the principle of differentiation of instruction in the language courses, with one special staff hired to teach grammatical analysis and another, to lead the oral practice sessions, the total sequence of instruction in a beginning language course is much influenced by the presence or absence of a "pre-reading period." Appendix A explains this practice and indicates how it stems from audio-lingual theory. The individual center inventories often specify the point at which reading is introduced in the course. For example: "The audio-lingual approach is predominant. Reading is introduced during the thirteenth week of the first year." Or again: "Since the spoken language is the goal on the elementary level, phonetic transcription is used. Reading and writing in traditional characters is postponed to the end of the first year."

The discussion of the prereading period at Conference V showed great variety in length: In the Harvard intensive Chinese course, the written symbols are introduced after two weeks of study; at Iowa, in the non-intensive course, at the fifteenth week; at Michigan, in the Japanese course, at the twelfth week; at Columbia, at the seventh week.

THE LANGUAGE LABORATORY

The inventory data show that at fifteen centers (or almost a third of the total group), laboratory facilities are poor. Either there was no laboratory or the facilities were very limited. But at 80 percent of these centers, a new laboratory was actually under construction at the time of our visit or was being planned for the immediate future. At sixteen centers (a little over a third), a laboratory is available to center students, tapes are prepared for them, and they are encouraged to use them. But, in our analysis of these centers, we decided that the laboratory is not actually an integral part of the center program, either because of insufficient physical facilities or lack of concern and/or knowledge on the part of the center staff. At the fifteen remaining centers (almost a third), there are good or excellent laboratory facilities available to center students, and laboratory work has been made an integral part of the language program.

Most of the centers do not have a laboratory of their own. Often a laboratory on a campus serves all language courses. Sometimes the laboratory actually belongs to one of the language departments and the center is invited to make use of it. Occasionally center staff do not have sufficient knowledge to take advantage of this invitation. "From the outset," one center director told our visitor, "the people in charge of the lab have welcomed us to use it. Our hesitation has come from our indecision as to just *how* to use it." Occasionally our data show that center students use the laboratory but the staff do not supervise the work done there. For example: "While there were 134 students registered in the lab to hear Russian tapes (of which 719 were played in one twenty-nine day period), often the technician did not know which tape to play unless the student informed him where they were in class."

All five of the conferences discussed the use of the laboratory in center language programs. *There was agreement that the significant function of the laboratory is to reinforce and make automatic what has already been presented in the classroom.* It is a mistake to assume that new materials can successfully be presented in a laboratory session.

Second, *it was agreed that the motivation to spend time in the laboratory is strongly related to the rewards the student receives by making better test grades and discovering in other ways that the laboratory drill is helping him attain the goals of the course more rapidly.* At Conference IV, the opinion was offered that for purposes of motivation, laboratory attendance should not have to be required— just as study hours in the library are not required of college students. On the other hand, since laboratory space is often at a premium, the most efficient way to make maximum utilization of laboratory space is to schedule students in it on a regular basis.

Third, *laboratory drills must be intimately related to classroom activities and to the texts required for study.* It is obvious that the laboratory work cannot be successful unless it is closely correlated with work done in the classroom. Experts in the field emphasized this point again and again at the conferences.

Our inventory shows that not all of the centers which are strongly committed in principle to the audio-lingual approach have language laboratory work integrally tied into their program. Nevertheless our data suggest, as one might expect, that *there is a positive relationship between commitment to audio-lingual principles and the use of the language laboratory.* Tables 11, 12, and 13 (pages 89–91) present the exact evidence.

Future Life of the Centers

D URING ITS FIRST TWO years of implementation, the National Defense Education Act radically altered the center concept. As it became national in scope, the concept became more universal in meaning. A bond among the forty-six language and area centers came into being as they participated in a common national enterprise.

Important changes have taken place during this two-year period. Not only have many of the conditions changed that prevailed at the time the NDEA center program began, but also the pressures for the immediate establishment of centers, having been satisfied, disappeared. And by more than doubling the number of NDEA centers in the second year of the program, from nineteen to forty-six, still another dimension was added to the center concept. In spite of these rapidly and continually changing conditions, our inventory offers evidence that the dynamics of center activity have generated a set of standards by which a center may be appraised. These standards have, however, remained largely unformulated and, indeed, have only recently become discernible.

The academic profession now has the responsibility of utilizing these standards in any plans which it projects for the future life of language and area centers. During the first two years of NDEA it would not have been possible for the profession to evaluate the centers on any comparative basis. Many of them were experimental. Some of them were entirely new. But the time has now come, we believe, when judgments can be made and comparisons can prove fruitful for the future.

The forty-six individual inventory reports illustrate quite clearly that different centers have met success in different ways.

1. Some of the centers have concentrated on the problems of teaching

a second language effectively; and they have collected evidence that indicates their success in these efforts.

2. Some of the centers have been able to establish an extraordinarily close relationship between the language courses and area studies; and staff teamwork has made possible the development of a core of interdisciplinary courses as well.

3. Some of the centers, initially focusing attention only on the graduate student, have also been able to build a successful and significant program of undergraduate instruction; and they have found the expansion at each level to be of benefit to both levels.

4. Certain centers were able to fit into interuniversity programs and to respond affirmatively in other ways to long-range plans involving more than a single campus; and they have done so without fearing the loss of their integrity or individuality.

Those centers which have made progress in one or another of these ways automatically help set the standards for all centers. The profession can now put such standards to use in appraising the effectiveness of an old center or in delineating the requirements of a new one.

During the first two years, such an evaluative process was not appropriate. In the first years of the center program, almost any reasonable plan was worth exploring. But the intense experience of the period from 1959 to 1961 has provided a basis for future experimentation and a means for appraising the direction of center movement. Experiments need no longer begin from scratch; centers need no longer be planned without reference to center history. That history has now come into being, and it is impossible to ignore the accumulated data at hand.

The sections which follow are intended to illustrate the kinds of questions and answers that will determine the position the academic profession must assume in planning the future life of language and area centers. The sections deal with these questions:

1. Should the audio-lingual approach to the teaching of languages be further developed and encouraged at the NDEA centers?

2. What are the guidelines for maintaining proper balance between language instruction and area work in the related disciplines?

3. Should programs in the uncommonly taught languages on the undergraduate level be expanded?

4. To what extent should American universities assume additional training tasks in the national interest, and what step must now be taken to ensure long-range planning, national in scope, for the future of language and area studies on American campuses?

The Future Course for Language Teachers

The inventory data show that half of the 1960–61 NDEA language and area centers are either fully or largely committed in principle to the audio-lingual approach in the teaching of languages.

It is clear that the profession generally is moving toward an endorsement of the audio-lingual approach. On the secondary school level, a large-scale conversion to this methodological framework is already taking place. This process is being facilitated by NDEA title III funds, by the unusual opportunities for high school teachers of language through the title VI institute program, and by the availability, in the fall of 1961, of audio-lingual teaching materials in five languages for the secondary school level.[1]

On the college and university level, the movement toward adoption of this mode of language instruction is slower but it is clearly discernible. Two factors which have prevented the movement from gathering momentum are now being combated. The primary factor has been the critical lack of instructional and drill materials. Many teachers who are committed to the audio-lingual approach in principle have not been able to fulfill this commitment because adequate text and drill materials are not yet available in many languages. A great many instructional tools are now, however, being constructed by language and area center personnel and through special projects organized by the Modern Language Association and other professional societies, with funds supplied under the NDEA title VI research program.

A second factor is more elusive, but it remains potent. It is the oversimplified description of the audio-lingual approach now being disseminated by some members of the language teaching profession. In a serious intellectual community such descriptions can do great harm.

[1] For example, *The A-LM* [Audio-lingual Method] *Program: Level One Materials* (New York: Harcourt, Brace & World, Inc., 1961) is available for French, German, Italian, Russian, and Spanish.

The most significant sign of progress on both fronts, revealed in our inventory data, is the newly acquired prestige within the language teaching profession that now attaches to research in the methods of teaching languages effectively and in the preparation of classroom materials appropriate for the audio-lingual framework.

In a sense, therefore, the profession has won its most crucial battle. Most college and university language teachers may, if they wish, now focus their attention on the problem of effective second-language teaching without fear of losing status among their colleagues. We feel confident that adequate data on the central questions of language teaching methods and adequate materials to ensure success in the use of those methods will not be long delayed.

We feel it important to reiterate here that, in administering the center program, the Office of Education has taken no official position on this methodological question. Nor is it our opinion that it should do so in the future. The language teaching profession itself should assume responsibility for solving this problem.

The evidence accumulated thus far strongly suggests that the audio-lingual approach to language instruction, in the hands of competent teachers, results in a higher level of language competence than other approaches used by equally competent teachers. Further experimental data for the college level are now being accumulated, and early indications are that the evidence thus far collected will be corroborated.[2]

We recommend that the profession spare no effort in disseminating accurate information about the audio-lingual teaching approach as it applies to college and university language instruction, and, in

---

[2] The most recently compiled data, as yet unpublished, were presented to the Office of Education in a mimeographed report submitted in the fall of 1961. These data were collected at the University of Colorado, which has completed its first year of a two-year project (directed by George A. C. Scherer) financed by the Language Development Section of the Office of Education. Two evenly matched groups completed their first year of instruction in German last June, one taught in the traditional way and the other taught by means of the audio-lingual approach.

At the end of the first semester, the experimental group was superior in speaking and listening skills, while the traditional group was superior in reading and writing. At the end of the first year, however, the experimental group was *far superior* in listening and speaking and had also caught up with the traditional group in reading and writing skills, performing on exactly the same level on the tests given.

On other tests, the experimental group showed greater ease and fluency in reading; on a specially constructed sentence reaction time test, the results showed that the audio-lingual group was able to assimilate the meaning of the German far more rapidly than the traditional group.

In all, seventy-one different measures were used in this project.

addition, that it continue to foster the development of teaching and drill materials in the critical languages as well as in the commonly taught languages.

Moreover, as new language and area centers are established and as present ones are expanded, the profession must carry the additional responsibility of encouraging the extended use of the audio-lingual instructional framework in the new programs.

Language and Area in Balance

While there is no doubt in the minds of center directors that their centers may legally offer, beyond the training in language, instruction in other fields, there is considerable uncertainty as to the optimum balance between expansion in the area disciplines and expansion in language studies. Some directors, believing that the intent of the law was primarily to improve language instruction, established their centers accordingly. Other center directors saw in the law an opportunity to expand area studies primarily. No better illustration can be found, we believe, of the way local option operates where no general standards exist, for an area studies program determined only by local conditions and meeting only local needs is not likely to reflect a proper balance between language and area.

While it was beyond our inventory task, and outside the scope of this report, to define what is proper expansion in area work, it is not difficult to see that there are limits beyond which area expansion would be considered excessive. Further, once they are established, these limits must be made known nationally since they should apply equally to all centers. Conversely, where no area work has been added to the center offerings (a choice also open to center directors), we found this practice as deleterious to the total program as excessive expansion of the area offerings.

The inventory reports show how varied the balance is at present between area and language from one center to another. Center directors who are *language* men, we discovered, were less likely than *area* men to provide liberally for expansion in area offerings, and they often seemed to us less willing to see relationships between language and area or to perceive the values of interdisciplinary work. On the other hand, directors whose own disciplines were in area fields were more likely to be liberal in providing expansion in language work.

This difference bears some relationship, in all probability, to the fact that by law a center is required to include language training but is not required to include area training. Still, among language staffs more often than among area staffs, we found men who seemed to us excessively cautious and defensive, somewhat uncomfortable, we thought, in the glaring spotlight into which recent events have placed the teaching of languages. But we also knew that in recent years language professors have often been sacrificial victims in the academic community. And anyone sensitive to the course of affairs on American campuses could not have expected a very quick or easy adjustment to this newest variant of the Cinderella story. Moreover, these recent changes have created new alignments in the power structure on each campus; petty politics, we were reminded, flourish as richly in communities of scholars as in other social systems.

The balance between language and area is, in a sense, the core of a center's program, for it gives shape to its current activities and it suggests its future form. We refuse to accept the notion that the particular balance that happens to result from the peculiar combination of local conditions on a given campus is *ipso facto* the proper language-area balance for an NDEA center on that campus.

We recommend that steps be taken, through conferences and other media, to place before center staffs models of language-area balance which now exist among the forty-six centers. In this way, those responsible for center development on their own campuses will be better able to plan a program calculated to realize such a center's potential.

Expansion to Lower Levels of Instruction

With only four of the forty-six centers designed exclusively for undergraduate students, the center program as a whole has been clearly directed at the graduate level. This is where most of the work in the uncommonly taught languages had previously been done, and this is where the future college teachers of these languages must receive their professional training.

The case is logical, and the current emphasis on graduate programs appears to be justified. *Our analysis suggests, however, that the over-*

all plan for future center development should carry an increased emphasis on the undergraduate level.

Most students enter the center program at present after they have received the B.A. degree. They begin their study of an uncommonly taught language during their first graduate year. Typically, they spend half of their time during that year taking an elementary and an intermediate course in the language. All center personnel agree that it would be desirable if these students, upon entering a center as graduates, had had two or three years of language study.

Undergraduate center courses in area, as chapter 2 makes clear, already play an important role. Among other purposes, they serve as a kind of recruiting station for potential language and area center students. On campuses that offer such courses, undergraduates have an opportunity to study a non-Western civilization in fulfillment of a portion of their general education requirements. At Chicago, Columbia, Cornell, and Harvard, to name only four institutions, these courses constitute a part of the offerings of the NDEA center. It is clear that if such undergraduate offerings (in addition to those in language) are increased, students will be encouraged to begin their language and area work earlier in their college careers than is the case at present.

It would appear that little more need be done to set the stage for this development. Yet our analysis suggests that this downward expansion will not occur smoothly or soon unless the profession as a whole sees the advantages in such a policy and makes a concerted effort to carry it through.

The conferences yield interesting data: Representatives from the graduate centers said they found such a development desirable. Some of them said they would welcome it on their campuses if it occurred. But, with several notable exceptions, all of them indicated that no steps were envisaged for fostering it positively. Other representatives pointed out other difficulties. Undergraduate center courses are certain to run into stiff competition from other programs attracting or requiring the time of undergraduates. The recruitment problem in the uncommonly taught languages among undergraduates is acute; this was reported universally. Moreover, center personnel wondered whether the "sales campaigns," which they assured us must take place if such programs are to survive, should become the responsibility of the language and area professors, who are already in extremely short supply.

At three of the five conferences for representatives of the NDEA centers, *the recommendation was made that the Federal Government support undergraduate training in the uncommonly taught languages by means of incentive scholarships.* Perhaps in no other way can the acute problem of student recruitment among undergraduates be solved.

If language and area programs are eventually to become integral and self-supporting segments in university curricula, we anticipate that they will follow the normal curricular pattern in American higher education: an undergraduate major program supplies a basis for the graduate program and provides for its support. On campuses where both graduate and undergraduate programs exist—usually, as they do, within the same department—the expansion of the center program downward is, therefore, seriously to be considered.

We envisage a variety of means by which undergraduate area studies could be fostered, particularly in liberal arts colleges which have no graduate school. *It ought to prove possible for two or three undergraduate colleges situated close together to work cooperatively toward the development of a language and area program. In addition, we suggest the establishment of a number of one-man centers on undergraduate campuses, giving work in one non-Western language and perhaps several area courses.*

The history of the twenties, with the single non-Western scholar on the university campus who was subsequently replaced by a team of specialists, can now begin to be repeated on undergraduate campuses —with greater experience, however, and professional guidance.

Language and Area Training and the National Interest

Given the current international scene, it seems likely that established language and area programs may be asked to perform additional services in the national interest. In fact, at Conference IV, it was reported that three universities had already been approached by government agencies with requests for special programs in Arabic. The demands of the International Cooperation Administration (now the Agency for International Development), the Peace Corps, and other federal agencies with overseas programs will not soon disappear.

We should like, therefore, to raise three questions: Should a university be expected to serve as an academic "boot camp" to provide certain specific training programs outside its normal business of higher education? Should a university allow its own fundamental purposes to be altered to suit the needs of the national interest? If federal funds are accepted by a college or university on a contractual basis, what kind of control should the federal agency have over the program which it is supporting?

In the case of the language and area centers, our inventory data show that no control of any sort was imposed on any individual center. Federal assistance for these centers was given on some thirty campuses; and for all forty-six centers, the unqualified verdict was: "We have run our centers without interference of any kind."

Our inventory makes clear that under the NDEA center program, no university was expected or required to serve as a national boot camp for aspiring students of foreign languages. NDEA center funds have been invested in programs that already existed on various campuses, within, one assumes, the university's own conception of its purposes. Where a new center was actually established, it was built by university personnel in consonance with the university's stated purposes. Centers have in no way been requested to provide extracurricular language services or to carry on a language program as an adjunct activity to the regular degree programs which constitute part of the regular curriculum of the university. Hence, in the case of the NDEA centers, academic goals have been neither questioned nor upset.

But left to its own devices, a normal graduate program is a rather long, drawn-out affair, even (our inventory indicates) when the student's professional training is hastened by giving him a fellowship, relieving him of his part-time jobs, and enrolling him in intensive language courses, including summer intensive programs. Let us for a moment suppose that the national interest should demand that the entire process be revamped and streamlined. If this development seems unlikely in the case of the NDEA centers (and we must report it does), let us then suppose a similar demand being made upon the universities for purposes beyond those envisaged in title VI, for example, language and area training for the Peace Corps.

This problem was raised at four of the five conferences and discussed in some detail at two of them. Representatives at the conferences expressed three distinct points of view. One group—the least vocal—indicated that this kind of demand might prove a challenge for the universities and might, in unexpected ways, even be helpful in university development. This group expressed the belief that such programs did not run any further counter to university purposes than a multitude of applied research projects now commonly being carried on in the natural sciences on all of the larger campuses. A second, more vocal, group felt that the universities ought simply and firmly to say "No" to any such proposal. It was suggested by members of this group that the government ought to set up separate schools for such programs; there the curriculum could be organized to meet specific needs. In that way, they claimed, the government would get its job done more efficiently and the universities would continue to perform theirs.

The majority of the center representatives, however, seemed to feel that while universities could not be expected to take on, as part of their regular programs, any project that did not fit the purposes and framework of their regular curricula, there was no reason why such projects could not be organized and planned by universities as activities outside their regular programs. In such cases, the organization of the project and the instruction given would be planned to fit exactly the specific purposes of the special program.

We cannot predict the form of new pressures for language and area training to which American universities might be subjected in the future. We can assert, however, that in the case of the NDEA centers, the national interest and the purposes of American higher education have in no case been seen to be in conflict.

Indeed, as we have implied, the language and area program provides a rare example of almost total agreement between (*a*) a set of responsibilities which the universities have wished to assume, but have not, in every case, been able to finance, and (*b*) a set of responsibilities which a government agency has been eager to have the universities assume and which it has been authorized to help support.

The next step is clear. The future development of language and area centers must be planned on a long-range basis; further, such a plan must be national in scope. We recommend that a series of meetings be arranged where key representatives from the academic world, the business world, the Federal Government, and the educational foundations will decide how such a plan may best be drawn up.

The Future Life of the Centers

The authors of this report do not have to be persuaded that there is no single "right" way of organizing a center or planning its instructional program. We have seen that each university is by its very nature different, and we agree that the most efficient policy, in the long run, is to let each different center do its job differently.

But we are not content to let the matter rest there, for the inventory has given us additional data which cannot be ignored. Our analysis of these data has persuaded us that:

1. *The problem of language teaching methodology is no longer purely a matter of speculation.*
2. *The major clues to optimum language-area balance can now be communicated to those responsible for center planning.*
3. *The inordinate length of graduate programs in the uncommonly taught languages can be reduced for future students by a downward expansion of offerings into the undergraduate departments and by summer intensive language courses.*
4. *Cooperative planning on a long-range, nation-wide basis by the universities, the Federal Government, and the educational foundations is possible and desirable, and should begin immediately.*

The inventory has shown that a partnership between forty-six centers and the Office of Education has come into existence that is intimate and harmonious. And we would not wish that relationship disturbed. Moreover, we have analyzed the Office's policy of local option as one dictated by wisdom and crowned by success. And we would not wish that policy abandoned. But the inventory has also shown us that the NDEA center programs have generated their own standards and have created their own models. And we would not wish these overlooked or rejected. Quite the reverse. We are suggesting that as a matter of future policy, those standards be applied and those models be followed.

The Audio-lingual Approach in College and University Language Teaching

A T VARIOUS POINTS in the foregoing description, there are references to the audio-lingual approach in the teaching of a foreign language. Since no explanation of its methodological framework is given, we believe it advisable to outline its features here.

This definition of the audio-lingual approach is not to be taken as a polemic in its behalf. Nor is it, certainly, to be taken as an essay in the field of linguistics; it is, rather, an exposition in the field of educational method.

Spoken Language and Written Forms

Language teachers who use the audio-lingual approach in their classrooms accept the view that language is first of all a "spoken-heard" phenomenon, that it is primarily a system of communication which uses as its means the production and perception of sounds.

Such teachers, therefore, try not to confuse a given language with the particular system traditionally used for writing that language. Indeed, the word "language" is often defined by linguists so as to exclude any system of written or printed symbols. The teacher using the audio-lingual approach need not necessarily accept this definition of language; but he is careful, in any case, never to equate a given language with the written form of that language. Yet his view of language as, first of all, a spoken-heard phenomenon by no means implies that he denies the significance of the written language. He recognizes the immense importance of written documents in the history of civilization, and since he is often a student of literature as well as language, he is aware of the unique qualities of the printed word and of the immeasurable power and beauty that it can attain.

The teacher who is committed to the audio-lingual approach agrees with the linguistic scientist that one learns a language by learning to control the various elements of the system as they interrelate one with another—the units of sound, the units of sound patterns that carry meaning, and the characteristic ways in which these combine into larger entities. It is obvious that if there is a traditional system for writing the language, the good language pedagogue will teach this writing system.

The view is held by adherents of the audio-lingual approach that written forms should be taught after the student already knows the spoken forms. This conviction is based on both logical and psychological grounds. Audio-lingual theorists argue that it would be illogical to teach the writing system *before* the study of the spoken forms is begun since the former is a way of symbolically representing the latter. In view of the history and nature of the written forms, this argument runs, the logical progression is not, "Look at this written form and *pronounce* it thus," but rather, "Form X—which you already know orally and aurally—is *written* thus."

A second argument contends that it is psychologically unsound, in terms of learning theory, to teach both the spoken and written forms *simultaneously,* for the two learning tasks are very different. Control of both forms is attained more quickly if during the initial stages of language study the two tasks are tackled separately. Moreover, it is claimed, if the spoken language is learned first, it is possible to transfer the language facility so acquired to the written form; but experience has not demonstrated the reverse to be true.

Many audio-lingual theorists maintain that in the case of college students and other adult learners, some sort of visual reinforcement is desirable as an aid to learning the sounds and structures during the period before the traditional writing system is learned. For this purpose, many language teachers and textbooks use phonemic spelling. This is a special way of representing the sound units of the language. It is easy for students to learn; and it is also easy for them to unlearn when they are ready for the traditional writing system.

In all classrooms, then, in which the audio-lingual approach is the dominant one, the writing system traditionally used by the speakers

of the foreign language will be introduced some time after the initial
stage of the learning process has begun. In that second stage of instruction—and up to a given point, in subsequent stages—the student is taught how to read the printed form of only those lexical units
or linguistic structures that he already has under control. Courses following this method are, therefore, characterized by the presence of
what is called a "prereading period." The length of this period varies
for different languages. Even among teachers of the same language,
there is a difference of opinion as to optimum length. It seems, in
general, to run from about four to twelve weeks on the college level.
The shortest prereading period among the centers we visited was two
weeks; the longest, two semesters.

It is obvious that the prereading period can be shorter for a language like Spanish than for one like English or Chinese. The point is
to be stressed that mere *separation in time between the two tasks—
the initial step in the study of the language and the initial step in the
study of its writing system—is not a significant element in audio-
lingual practice. Seen pedagogically, the crux lies rather in the separation of the two tasks in the student's mind.* This separation helps him
master each of these seperate tasks more firmly; but in addition, it
disabuses him of the notion—reinforced by popular misconceptions—
that when he is learning the writing system, he is learning the language.

Theorists of the audio-lingual approach claim that when a language teacher follows these principles, his students (after, say, two
years of college study) are able to read the language more quickly
and with greater comprehension than equally intelligent students who
have studied the language by other methods under equally good teachers. Unfortunately the interpretation of the data thus far compiled on
this particular point is itself a subject of controversy; the audio-lingual
teachers claim that the case has been adequately demonstrated, while
others maintain it has not.

*It is generally regarded as indisputable that students taught by the
audio-lingual approach are able to attain a greater speaking and listening ability in a shorter time than students taught by any other approach. Still it remains significant that audio-lingual theorists and
teachers are not content merely with this admission of their partial
superiority. They insist that their approach is the most effective one*

for all purposes—whether the student's immediate or long-run goals include the speaking-listening abilities, or whether they are limited to the reading goal alone.

The New Conception of Language Drill
in Classroom and Laboratory

When a teacher accepts the view of language as a system of communication whose primary means are the production and perception of sounds, then certain pedagogical implications follow. The preceding section attempted to analyze some of these implications.

There is a second characterization about language that the audio-lingual teacher accepts and that has equally great pedagogical implications. This is the notion of language as a system of responses that have been so well learned as to have become habitual.

The adherent of the audio-lingual approach not only accepts this characterization as true (indeed, no one can dispute it) but makes it a cornerstone of his method. It is this principle that accounts for the extraordinary amount of drill that the inventory project visitors witnessed whenever we visited a drill session in a course based on audio-lingual principles. This principle not only accounts for the enormous amount of drill, but also, in large part, for the kind of drill exercises that are typically used. They must be the sort which will lead to responses that are automatic.

For example, let us imagine that a native speaker of English begins to say, "John believes in ghosts," but interrupts himself after a syllable or two because he wishes to express himself more exactly. John's belief, the speaker wants to be sure to convey, is not limited to the present time only; indeed, on the matter of ghosts, John has never had any other belief. This is what the speaker decides he wants to say. In an instant he restates his point, now selecting the structure "John has always believed in ghosts."

The change has not been a simple one. Merely adding the word "always" to the sentence "John believes in ghosts" would not sufficiently have conveyed the meaning. Nor would the mere change of "believes" to "has believed" have conveyed it. Both changes were necessary. Yet the entire process took place in an instant. The selection of the appropriate linguistic forms, once the speaker was clear about what he wanted to say, was completely automatic. He did not mentally call up any verb charts nor did he have to reason from a rule of grammar to a particular case in order to make the selection of the forms he needed.

The automatic response that is characteristic of linguistic behavior in one's mother tongue is also the goal of the audio-lingual classroom in a foreign language. The drill exercises are accordingly designed toward that goal.

The audio-lingual theorist contends that if students at an early stage in their language training are habitually encouraged or directed to translate linguistic structures from one language to another by reasoning out the correct translation on the basis of rules, it is self-evident that such exercises will not build toward automatic response as effectively as the kinds of drill in which analysis and ratiocination are minimized or eliminated altogether. Analysis plays an important role in the audio-lingual approach in college and university classrooms, but during the drill sessions the person in charge—whether language teacher or drill master—makes every attempt to minimize it.

Linguistic analysis enables a student to understand precisely how a strange structure in a foreign tongue differs from one in his own language; but analysis alone cannot lead the student's ear to feel the foreign structure as natural. Only repeated drill can have this effect. Indeed, as long as the student continues to feel a given language pattern is strange, he knows that he has not yet mastered it.

Here, perhaps, lies the key to the reason for the unexpected success which audio-lingual teachers claim to have had in teaching their students to read. If the verb at the end of a dependent clause in German, for example, is exactly where the audio-lingually trained student feels it naturally belongs, he is not likely, in reading, to waste time looking for it before he gets to it. The drill session is responsible for building habits that lead to smoothness and ease in reading.

There appear to be three major features of an audio-lingual drill session. The first, as we have seen, is the unusual amount of drill in classes using the audio-lingual approach when they are compared with classes using other methods. Sessions of straight drill typically take three-fifths of the total class time.

Second, the drill material emphasizes forms and structures in the foreign language that contrast with forms and structures in the mother tongue. The exercises not only stress sharply contrastive structures—for example, English "I have a book" as contrasted with Russian "To me, book"—but they also provide ways of combating interference from forms and structures in the mother tongue that are similar but not identical with those in the foreign language. Scholars in the field of applied linguistics tell us that such patterns are, in many cases, harder to master than the totally alien.

Third, the exercises are constructed so that language patterns are repeated over and over again. (A language pattern is a characteristic way in which the language combines its sound units and lexical units into complete entities that carry meaning.) The student is not so much asked to repeat a given sentence over and over again as he is asked to repeat the pattern over and over again.

The student is expected to master the pattern by being asked, for example, in sequentially built exercises (which are presented orally and rapidly) to fill different "slots" of the pattern with different particular items. In such exercises, when a new "filler" is placed in a given slot of the pattern, the other items which have remained in the other slots may (or may not) also change. The student must learn to make these other changes (or not to make them) automatically. For example, in the sentence "I'm studying Twi," if the particular item now filling the first slot is changed from "I" to *any other item* that English permits in that slot (for it allows only certain kinds of fillers to enter that slot), then the filler which is now in the second slot of that sentence must also change. This change is required by an element of the English language system that we all have learned as the grammatical rule of agreement between subject and verb. But a knowledge of the rule generally describing this aspect of English structure is in itself not sufficient. Only intensive drill can *fix* the forms so deeply that responses on the part of the student are automatic.

Such exercises, performed orally and rapidly in the classroom, are a characteristic feature of every language class that uses the audio-lingual approach. It is in connection with this kind of drill that the language laboratory can play its most important role. *If one can assume that appropriate drill material is selected or constructed for the tapes used in the laboratory, the laboratory presents the most efficient —and, in the long run, most economical—means of deepening the student's control of materials over which classroom sessions can give him partial but not total mastery.*

At a number of the language and area centers, we observed special drill sessions led by instructional assistants called "drill masters." After these assistants have accumulated considerable skill and experience, and only then, are they themselves permitted to construct or select the drill materials which they use. New material, however, is generally not taught to the students by the drill masters; only a professionally trained language teacher is able to present the new material for a given lesson or unit. Only he has the training to construct or select drill materials or to supervise their construction or selection, whether for use in the classroom drill session or in the laboratory.

As the audio-lingual approach is now practiced on college and university campuses that are fully committed to it, the construction of drill exercises and their recording for use in the laboratory are never assigned as incidental activities to be done by a language teacher in his spare time. These constitute major responsibilities.

In this conception of the exercises that characterize the drill sessions lies the major distinction between the audio-lingual approach and an older, very popular, approach to language teaching called "the direct method." The direct-method teacher insists that the student's mother tongue never be used. The teacher communicates meanings by pointing to objects, acting out sentences, engaging in exaggerated gestures, and so on. As the student's listening skill grows, the teacher uses the foreign language increasingly, but the charade element in the method continues to some extent since all use of the mother tongue is forbidden. Second, the direct-method teacher gives no explanations of any sort, not even to adult students. Language analysis plays no part in his pedagogic process. Third, the major classroom medium upon which he depends is structured conversation; he does not typically ask his students to go through the type of drill just described.

Theorists of the audio-lingual school deny kinship with the direct method.[1]

[1] See Nelson Brooks, *Language and Language Learning* (New York: Harcourt, Brace & World, Inc., 1960), who does so explicitly on pp. 207–8.

The New Conception of the Professional
Language Teacher as "Analyst"

For more mature students (beginning perhaps with the late high school years, but in any case including college students), it is usually considered advisable to schedule class sessions for language analysis in addition to those designed for language drill.

These two major instructional activities are, however, generally not carried on during the same period. Courses organized on the principles underlying the audio-lingual approach tend to separate sharply those class activities designed to build automatic response (described in the preceding section) from those class activities which develop the student's understanding of the language system he is studying. These latter activities are of an analytic nature, completely different from the former, pedagogically, in purpose and form. They involve explanation, analysis, and other intellectual processes. There is, indeed, a complex body of material to organize and present, and only highly trained personnel can carry out these functions effectively.

Because these two kinds of language-learning activities are different in purpose and form, it has been found more economical to differentiate between them, both in the class schedule drawn up for students and in the assignments made to staff. In a course meeting five hours per week, analysis sessions commonly take one or two hours. Drill sessions are, of course, kept small, but the analysis sessions are often quite large.

While English is the language in which the analysis class is taught, it is considered desirable to have a native speaker available during the analysis sessions. It is often considered an advantage to have a model of native speech other than the analyst, even if the latter happens to be a native speaker of the language under discussion. The reasons seem to be, first, that it is good for ear training to vary models; and, second, that it is psychologically sounder if the analyst always uses the mother tongue and the native speaker, the foreign language. (However, in our center visits, we often observed a native-speaking teacher presenting the grammatical analysis and also serving as his own model. Occasionally we found such a teacher's English inadequate to communicate the complexities of his subject matter. And his services as a model did not appear to us to compensate for his ineffectiveness as a teacher.) If a model other than the analysis teacher is used, he is usually referred to as an "informant." Often the same individual serves also as a drill master. But his function in these two capacities is very different.

The analysis session, then, is carried on by someone qualified by training and aptitude to teach linguistic analysis. In addition, it is his responsibility to select or construct the materials for the drill sessions and the laboratory. But it is unnecessarily expensive and it is inefficient, the audio-lingual theorists argue, for this highly qualified language teacher to be assigned to lead drill sessions. Occasionally, of course, local conditions make such an assignment necessary.

Whenever circumstances permit, therefore, a language department committed to the audio-lingual approach appoints special staff as drill masters; this appointment is generally at the rank of assistant instructor since no professional training is required. The drill master should, of course, be a native speaker, but there is no reason why he need have had any previous training in linguistics. However, where he has not had experience or training as a drill master, it is generally agreed, a period of in-service training is indispensable.

A significant feature of the audio-lingual approach as it is often practiced on the college level, then, is the division of labor in the instructional process, with analyst, drill master, and linguistic informant each responsible for different tasks.

How the Language Professor Explains Linguistic Phenomena

The analysis sessions in an audio-lingual language class have three identifying marks. First, the instructor presents the foreign language as it is actually used by educated people in their day-by-day lives. He avoids, insofar as he can, presenting the language as traditional grammarians conceive it *ought* to be spoken; and he avoids presenting the language as it is used only on formal occasions, for example, in formal addresses. For different languages this principle presents different kinds of problems. The teacher of Arabic, for example, must look with envy at the situation in which teachers of some European languages find themselves, where there is a single, standard language that all educated speakers more or less use in their daily lives. At the same time a standard language tends to be heavily surrounded by prescriptions issuing from academies dedicated to keeping the language pure, and the audio-lingual instructor tries to keep himself from being contaminated by them.

This point has by now become a *cause célèbre* among descriptive linguists—with its motto which places "describe" and "prescribe" in deadly opposition—so that nothing further probably need be added here except to say that the audio-lingual teacher appears to take this principle seriously. For example, he characteristically insists that the speed of utterances in the foreign language, even from the very beginning of his elementary course, be within the normal range for native speakers. He is constantly on guard against slowing down when he uses the foreign language with his students, and if he does slow down at any time, he does so with full awareness and for special reasons; and in the process he tries not to distort the characteristic sound patterns of the language.

The problem of speed, however, is simple compared to the selection of vocabulary and structure. Just as one tends to slow down and distort his speech when he is talking to a foreigner, so he tends even more to select special vocabulary and structures for the foreigner. A professor in a college, speaking to a colleague in the faculty club, might quite naturally say, "Did you get the stuff we talked about yesterday?" but there exists the danger that in his foreign language classroom (assuming English to be the foreign language in this example), the same speaker might be tempted to select special vocabulary and a more formal structure: "Did you obtain the material about which we spoke yesterday?" This is the sentence which, for some reason, a native English speaker *expects the foreigner to use.* Native-speaking teachers of a foreign language often tend to teach their students the language they expect foreigners to use rather than the one they themselves naturally use in their day-by-day conversations with other educated people.[2] The audio-lingual teacher is aware of this tendency and does what he can to combat it.

[2] We submit, in evidence of this point, an observation by Y. R. Chao. He notes (*Language*, XXIX [1953], 406) that an American reviewer of his *Mandarin Primer* (*Harvard Journal of Asiatic Studies*, XIII [1950], 241) called its language "almost slangishly idiomatic." But according to Chao, it merely reproduced the speech used "when I and my fellow Chinese professors of Chinese talk Chinese in China."

A second identifying mark of audio-lingual analysis sessions concerns the teacher's attitude toward linguistic description. He has had enough training in linguistics to know that statements cannot be defended which assert that, for example, one language is intrinsically easy while another is hard; that one has a rich vocabulary while another has not; that one is musical while another is guttural; that one is lucid while another is subtle and a third is ponderous; or that one native speaker has a beautiful accent while another has an ugly one. Such statements are, of course, commonly made, and when he hears his students make them, the audio-lingual teacher neither ignores them nor finds them meaningless, but tries to show how they may reveal deep-seated psychological states or social attitudes on the part of the speaker.

In any case, such statements do not describe language; and the audio-lingual practitioner avoids such phrases himself in daily conversation and tries to show his students why they are inappropriate in any objective description of language, such as he himself attempts to give in the analysis class sessions.

Third, the language professor who accepts audio-lingual principles prefers to explain the structures of the foreign language in terms of the self-consistent system of which they are a part. He does not usually present reasons (or encourage his students to seek them) which are outside of the language system itself.

It goes without saying that explanations and analyses of linguistic phenomena are possible on many levels and from many points of view, but the adherent of the audio-lingual approach appears to believe that all such frameworks—except one—are irrelevant to his particular purpose in the language analysis classroom. The one framework pertinent to his task, he believes, analyzes the specifics of the structure in terms of their place in the total system. For example, suppose a Chinese student of English becomes aware that English uses a complex system of verb modifications to make time relationships explicit, even when the time element may not be significant to either the speaker or the person to whom he is speaking. (In English sentences, an event cannot simply "occur"; it occurs or is occurring or does occur or occurred or has occurred or had occurred or will occur or will have occurred or would occur or was occurring or has been occurring or had been occurring or will have been occurring or used to occur, etc.) The Chinese student asks why English has this feature.

The only reason which the typical audio-lingual practitioner will give to account for this or any other particular feature is that it is an integral element in a total, self-consistent system. To say that the feature has the shape it does because the system requires it is admittedly not very much of an explanation. But it is as much explanation as the audio-lingual language instructor needs to give in order to attain his pedagogic goals.

Rather commonly, however, one hears explanations given in the college classroom which go outside the current system of the language being taught. For example, often linguistic change is used to explain certain forms and structures; and in this process the instructor will point to a causal relationship between the current system being studied and some other language system. Many language teachers hold that beyond this, no further explanation is possible, since the elemental sound units and structural units of a language have a necessary connection only with one another or with another language system.

The audio-lingual instructor at the present time appears to be cautious with respect to explanations that go beyond the system of the language being studied. The most common category of such explanations is that which accounts for specific items in the language system by finding the cause in some non-linguistic phenomenon.

In one Chinese class we visited, for example, the instructor explained why English uses a complex system of verb modifications to make time relationships explicit, even when this datum is not significant to the speaker or the hearer, and why this is not the case in Chinese. Native speakers of English, he said, in both thought and action, characteristically bind their lives tightly to the time dimension, whereas speakers of Chinese do not. The instructor was rather excited about this idea and at one point in his exposition, we thought, was on the verge of positing the more daring hypothesis that the modes of thought, far from accounting for the linguistic structures in the two languages, were indeed themselves determined by those structures.

If the instructor had reached that point, he would have entered a field that many linguists have come to refer to as "metalinguistics." The audio-lingual language teacher, however keen his interest in such problems may be, characteristically refrains from discussing them in his regular language classes. *In his capacity as language analyst, he explains to his students what the structures of the foreign language are and how they contrast with those of the students' mother tongue; but he considers it irrelevant to his task—and indeed, undesirable or even impossible—to explain why they are as they are, except to show how they function as part of a total system whose parts are intimately interrelated.* He believes that the more analytically descriptive he is, the more useful he will be to his students.

Center Statistics

IN THE TABLES THAT FOLLOW, we have tried to synthesize into concise statistical form the mass of quantitative data collected by the project visitors. Habitual readers of tables that present educational data will not need to be reminded of the care that must be taken in reading them. Such a reader, for example, in perusing enrollment statistics in language courses, knows that the same student may be taking two, or possibly even three, language courses during the same semester; a student majoring in the language very probably would. Hence, when the reader finds "290 enrollments" in a given language for the autumn semester, he must remember that this does not necessarily mean 290 different students studied the language during that semester.

On the other hand, he must also remember that while a student enrolled in a language course that meets three times per week counts as *one* enrollment, a student in an intensive language course meeting nine hours per week also counts as one enrollment. Caution must, therefore, be used in making comparisons on the basis of enrollment data alone. Some educational administrators, indeed, recommend the device of multiplying the number of enrollments by the number of credit hours or by the number of contact hours; in that way comparisons, they claim, may more validly be made.

But contact-hour figures create their own problems: Are we to include the hours spent in the laboratory? Is a course with six contact hours yielding six credit hours to be regarded as equivalent to another course with six contact hours yielding four credit hours? Are three hours of grammatical analysis and five hours of drill per week equivalent to five hours of grammatical analysis and three hours of drill? (Both schemes are common for eight-hour-per-week intensive language courses.)

In similar manner, the system of multiplying the number of enrollments by the number of credit hours also creates as many problems as it solves. Moreover, we felt that for most readers the easiest statistic to read and

[76]

understand, so far as enrollments are concerned, is the straight enrollment figure.

Similar problems exist in the case of statistics about course offerings. Again, an intensive course, yielding eight credit hours, counts as one course; two non-intensive courses, each yielding four credit hours, count as two. Furthermore, just as the same student may count as two enrollments, so sometimes may the same course count as two "offerings." Twi 1 and Twi 101, it may turn out, were given by the same instructor in the same room at the same time on the same days of the week. Both are elementary courses; undergraduates registered for Twi 1, graduates for Twi 101. Technically, these are two different course offerings.

This numbering practice seems to be disappearing on many campuses but it still exists sufficiently, we discovered, to plague the compiler of statistical data. A similar practice involving course names is also fairly common on some campuses among area courses—Political Science 185 turns out to be identical with International Relations 185. In compiling the figures presented on the following pages, we made every effort to eliminate such duplications, but we do not know how far we succeeded.

If a language course was offered but had no takers, should it be counted as a "course offering"? Technically the course was offered even though, as matters turned out, it was not given. We decided to count only the language courses actually *given*, and our column headings in the tables make this explicit.

Likewise, Table 1, listing the NDEA centers, shows the languages actually taught at each center during the autumn semester 1960. Table 1 is, therefore, not identical in every detail with the list of center languages offered in 1960–61 which was issued by the Office of Education.[1]

In studying Tables 2–5, which deal with center staff size, the reader may wonder what principle we followed in counting faculty members. If a faculty member served on the language staff of a center and also on the area staff, did we count him as two staff members? It seems obvious that he should be counted only once, and this was, therefore, our practice. An alternative would have been to determine his exact division of time between language and area, and count him, for example, .667 on one list and .333 on the other; but we came to the conclusion that this solution was not feasible.

---

[1] *Language and Area Centers: Report on the First Two Years,* Language Development Program, Title VI, National Defense Education Act of 1958, U.S. Office of Education Publication OE-56002 (Washington: U.S. Dept. of Health, Education, and Welfare, 1960), pp. 4–8.

A four-year report on language and area centers will be issued by the Office of Education in 1962.

Nor was it feasible to include in our count center staff below the rank of instructor. In accordance with that decision, Tables 2–5 do not show the large number of language teaching assistants at the NDEA centers— drill masters, informants, and others. A footnote to Table 2 does present the basic figures about them, however.

Most of these instructional assistants serve on a part-time basis. It would not have been possible to translate these part-time posts into full-time equivalents. But even if we had wished to add time fractions, the total would have been virtually meaningless. The term "half-time," for example, when applied to an instructional assistant means quite different duties and teaching loads on different campuses; even within the very same NDEA center (according to one of our inventory reports), the "half-time" assistants who had classes of their own carried a load anywhere from four hours weekly to seven or eight.

The statistical tables quite naturally presuppose some knowledge about the centers. We assume, for example, that in reading Table 7, which concerns the availability of interdisciplinary degree programs and certificate programs at the centers, the reader would not need a footnote explaining what certificate programs are, since this is explained in the body of the report; nor should he have to be told that this particular table *excludes* degree programs in a single discipline granted by the center or by one of its constituent units.

Further, in reading the same table, if he sees that an interdisciplinary doctoral program is available through a given center, he should know from chapter 2 that he would be fairly safe in assuming the availability of an interdisciplinary master's program through the same center; but he would not be safe in assuming that an interdisciplinary bachelor's degree is available through the center, since he knows from the body of the report that while some of the graduate centers have jurisdiction over bachelor's degrees, many do not.

A word should be said about the tables that attempt to quantify non-objective data. Table 12, for example, reports the number of centers at which the laboratory is or is not integrated with the center language program. This and the other judgments reflected in that table (as also in Table 11, regarding the centers' commitment to the audio-lingual approach) were made only after considering a large variety of evidence: the individual inventory for each center, which contains a good deal of descriptive material about the use of the laboratory and about practices in the language classes; the teaching materials which were collected by the Inventory visitor and sent to project headquarters with his report; and the discussions at the conferences called by the project for representatives of the centers. In addition, every judgment made for Tables 11 and 12 was checked with the project visitors to the centers.

All of the tables carefully carry a time designation—"Autumn 1960." This is because we are so conscious of the fact that these statistical data are already obsolete. For example, of the fifteen centers which in the autumn semester 1960 had no language laboratory at all or very limited (often borrowed) facilities, it is likely that twelve will have fairly adequate or even excellent facilities by the time these words appear in print. Where our inventory data showed definite plans for the immediate future —as in the cases of language laboratories, where funds must be authorized in advance and a date for completion is set—we have tried to reflect these plans in the tables.

The tables of Appendix B have been arranged in logical sequence. The reader finds in Table 1 a listing of the centers, with the languages given at each during the autumn semester 1960 and the amount of federal support for 1960–61. He then moves to a group of three tables presenting the size of the teaching staffs at the centers, and then he finds Table 5 comparing the size of language staffs and area staffs.

The next two tables deal with the relationship between the center and the disciplines which contribute to its life: Table 6 reports on the organization of the center, and Table 7 indicates the availability of interdisciplinary degree or certificate programs through the centers.

Tables 8–10 deal with enrollment figures and with course offerings for the language side of the center programs. Following this purely quantitative material about the work in language, the next three tables, 11–13, referred to earlier, attempt to quantify three important questions: the first reports the degree of center commitment to the audio-lingual approach; the second concerns the degree to which a laboratory serves as an integral part of the program; and the third explores the relationship between the audio-lingual commitment and laboratory use.

Following these data about the language side of the center program, Table 14 gives the number of course offerings in area studies, classifying the offerings within disciplines or, for those courses which are not given in a discipline department or do not fall into a single discipline, as interdisciplinary.

Finally, the list is completed by two tables which deal with student population data at the centers. Table 15 presents the number of degree and certificate candidates taking either a major or minor program at the centers. Table 16 presents the number of graduate students at the centers receiving scholarship and fellowship aid.

TABLE 1

NDEA Language and Area Centers, with Languages Given in Autumn, 1960, and Amount of Federal Support for 1960–61

Institution	Languages Given Autumn, 1960		Federal Matching Funds
	With Federal Support	Without Federal Support	
University of Arizona Language and Area Center for Oriental Studies	Chinese, Japanese, Hindi		$20,625
University of California, Berkeley South Asia Language and Area Center	Hindi-Urdu, Persian, Telugu	Sanskrit	47,009
University of California, Berkeley East European Language and Area Center	Russian, Polish, Serbo-Croatian, Hungarian	Czech	39,527
University of California, Los Angeles African Language and Area Center	Swahili, Kpelle		20,991
University of California, Los Angeles Near Eastern Language and Area Center	Arabic, Berber, Modern Hebrew, Persian, Turkish, Ethiopic: Amharic, Geez, Tigrinya	Armenian, Ugaritic	43,663
University of Chicago Far Eastern Language and Area Center	Chinese, Japanese		21,700
University of Chicago South Asia Language and Area Center	Hindi-Urdu, Bengali	Sanskrit	65,082
University of Colorado East European Language and Area Center	Russian, Czech, Polish, Hungarian		24,797
Columbia University Soviet and East European Language and Area Center	Russian, Czech, Polish, Serbo-Croatian, Slovak	Lithuanian, Rumanian	37,996
Columbia University East Asian Language and Area Center	Chinese, Japanese		22,509
Columbia University Uralic-Altaic Language and Area Center	Hungarian, Finnish, Estonian, Turkish, Uzbek, Mongolian		52,764
Cornell University South Asia Language and Area Center	Hindi-Urdu		28,000
Cornell University Southeast Asia Language and Area Center	Burmese, Indonesian-Malay, Thai, Vietnamese		50,000
Cornell University East Asia Language and Area Center	Chinese, Japanese		22,000

Institution	Languages		Amount
DUQUESNE UNIVERSITY African Language and Area Center	Swahili		$15,634
FORDHAM UNIVERSITY Russian Language and Area Center	Russian		23,371
HARVARD UNIVERSITY Language and Area Center for East Asian Studies	Chinese, Japanese, Korean	Mongolian, Tibetan	49,379
HARVARD UNIVERSITY Center for Middle Eastern Studies	Arabic, Hebrew, Persian, Turkish	Armenian	52,577
HARVARD UNIVERSITY Slavic Language and Area Center	Russian, Bulgarian, Czech, Polish, Serbo-Croatian, Ukrainian		38,802
UNIVERSITY OF HAWAII Language and Area Center in Chinese and Japanese	Chinese, Japanese	Korean	21,232
UNIVERSITY OF HAWAII Language and Area Center in Indonesian and Thai	Indonesian, Thai		10,350
HOWARD UNIVERSITY African Language and Area Center	Swahili, Yoruba		8,091
UNIVERSITY OF ILLINOIS Center for Russian Language and Area Studies	Russian		49,992
INDIANA UNIVERSITY Slavic Language and Area Center	Russian, Polish, Serbo-Croatian		50,000
STATE UNIVERSITY OF IOWA Chinese Language and Area Center	Chinese		10,177
JOHNS HOPKINS UNIVERSITY Near East Language and Area Center	Arabic		12,559
UNIVERSITY OF KANSAS East Asian Language and Area Center	Chinese		14,015
UNIVERSITY OF MICHIGAN Far Eastern Language and Area Center	Chinese, Japanese		23,609
UNIVERSITY OF MICHIGAN Language and Area Center for Near Eastern Studies	Arabic, Persian, Turkish	Hindi, Hebrew, Sanskrit, Ugaritic	36,590
UNIVERSITY OF MICHIGAN Slavic Language and Area Center	Russian, Polish		70,419
MICHIGAN STATE UNIVERSITY African Language and Area Center	Yoruba		25,759

TABLE 1—*continued*

Institution	Languages Given Autumn, 1960		Federal Matching Funds
	With Federal Support	Without Federal Support	
NEW YORK UNIVERSITY Portuguese Language and Area Center	Portuguese		$49,012
UNIVERSITY OF PENNSYLVANIA South Asia Language and Area Center	Hindi-Urdu, Marathi, Tamil	Pali, Sanskrit	72,162
UNIVERSITY OF PENNSYLVANIA Slavic Language and Area Center	Russian, Polish, Serbo-Croatian	Lettish	38,964
UNIVERSITY OF PITTSBURGH Chinese Language and Area Center	Chinese		17,934
PORTLAND STATE COLLEGE Middle East Studies Center	Arabic, Hebrew		25,019
PRINCETON UNIVERSITY Center for Middle Eastern Studies	Arabic, Persian, Turkish	Hebrew, Sanskrit, Ugaritic	51,462
UNIVERSITY OF SOUTHERN CALIFORNIA Soviet-Asian Studies Center	Chinese, Russian	Japanese	26,080
STANFORD UNIVERSITY Chinese-Japanese Language and Area Center	Chinese, Japanese		40,360
UNIVERSITY OF TEXAS South Asia Language and Area Center	Hindi, Telugu	Sanskrit	10,344
UNIVERSITY OF TEXAS Near Eastern Language and Area Center	Arabic		25,038
UNIVERSITY OF UTAH Middle Eastern Language and Area Center	Arabic, Hebrew, Persian, Turkish		36,510
UNIVERSITY OF WASHINGTON Far Eastern and Russian Language and Area Center	Chinese, Japanese, Russian, Mongolian, Tibetan	Korean Serbo-Croatian	68,610
UNIVERSITY OF WISCONSIN South Asia Language and Area Center	Hindi, Telugu	Sanskrit	40,791
UNIVERSITY OF WISCONSIN Luso-Brazilian Language and Area Center	Portuguese		32,810
YALE UNIVERSITY Southeast Asia Studies Center	Burmese, Vietnamese	Indonesian	30,685

TABLE 2

Size of Instructional Staffs at the NDEA Language and Area Centers: Language Faculty,* Autumn, 1960

Number of Faculty Members Teaching Language Courses	Centers, Classified by Area							
	African	Far Eastern	Far Eastern in Combination with South Asian or Slavic	Luso-Brazilian	Near and Middle Eastern	Slavic, East European, and Uralic-Altaic	South and Southeast Asian	Total
15 or more...			1			3		4
11–14.........		2			1	1		4
7–10..........		3			3	3	1	10
4– 6..........		2	2	2	1	3	4	14
1– 3..........	4	3			3		4	14
Total....	4	10	3	2	8	10	9	46

* Numbers include only members of instructional staffs teaching language in the centers who hold the rank of instructor or above. Those not on the NDEA budget are included as well as those who are. Excluded are instructional assistants—informants, drill masters, laboratory assistants, teaching assistants, teaching associates. These are typically part-time employees. Seven of the forty-six centers have no such assistants. For the thirty-nine which do, the range runs from one to twenty-six, and the average number per center (for these thirty-nine) is almost exactly five.

TABLE 3

Size of Instructional Staffs at the NDEA Language and Area Centers: Area Faculty,* Autumn, 1960

Number of Faculty Members Teaching Area Courses	Centers, Classified by Area							
	African	Far Eastern	Far Eastern in Combination with South Asian or Slavic	Luso-Brazilian	Near and Middle Eastern	Slavic, East European, and Uralic-Altaic	South and Southeast Asian	Total
15 or more...		1				1	1	3
11–14.........	1	2	1		1	1	3	9
7–10..........		2	1	1	2	4	1	11
4– 6..........	2	3		1	2	1	1	10
0– 3..........	1	2	1		3	3	3	13
Total....	4	10	3	2	8	10	9	46

* Excluded are instructors of courses in literature, even when such courses are given in English, as such staff members are invariably also language faculty and hence included in Table 2. Figures include only instructors in area courses reported in the individual center inventories to have a formal relationship to the center program and listed as center area staff.

TABLE 4

SIZE OF INSTRUCTIONAL STAFFS AT THE NDEA LANGUAGE AND AREA CENTERS:
LANGUAGE AND AREA FACULTY COMBINED,* AUTUMN, 1960

NUMBER OF FACULTY MEMBERS TEACHING IN THE CENTER	CENTERS, CLASSIFIED BY AREA							
	African	Far Eastern	Far Eastern in Combination with South Asian or Slavic	Luso-Brazilian	Near and Middle Eastern	Slavic, East European, and Uralic-Altaic	South and Southeast Asian	Total
21 or more...	....	3	1	....	....	1	1	6
16–20.......	....	....	....	....	3	4	3	10
11–15.......	1	3	1	1	1	3	1	11
6–10.......	1	3	1	1	1	2	2	11
1– 5.......	2	1	....	....	3	....	2	8
Total....	4	10	3	2	8	10	9	46

* Numbers include only members of instructional staffs holding the rank of instructor or above. Those not on the NDEA budget are included as well as those who are. Instructional assistants are excluded. See also footnotes, Tables 2 and 3.

TABLE 5

COMPARATIVE SIZE OF LANGUAGE STAFFS AND AREA STAFFS AT THE NDEA
LANGUAGE AND AREA CENTERS,* AUTUMN, 1960

COMPARATIVE SIZE	CENTERS, CLASSIFIED BY AREA							
	African	Far Eastern	Far Eastern in Combination with South Asian or Slavic	Luso-Brazilian	Near and Middle Eastern	Slavic, East European, and Uralic-Altaic	South and Southeast Asian	Total
Area staff exceeds language staff								
By 1– 3 members...........	1	2	.....	1	3	4	1	12
By 4– 7 members...........	1	4	1	.....	.....	.....	1	7
By 8–12 members...........	1	1	.....	.....	.....	.....	.....	2
By more than 12 members...	.....	.....	.....	.....	.....	.....	2	2
Language staff equals area staff	.....	.....	.....	1	1	.....	2	4
Language staff exceeds area staff								
By 1– 3 members...........	1	2	1	.....	2	2	3	11
By 4– 7 members...........	.....	.....	.....	.....	2	1	.....	3
By 8–12 members...........	.....	.....	.....	.....	.....	.....	.....	.....
By more than 12 members...	.....	1	1	.....	.....	3	.....	5†
Total...................	4	10	3	2	8	10	9	46

* Excluding instructional assistant; see Table 2, footnote asterisk.
† Three of these five are centers located completely within a language and literature department, and a fourth is located almost completely within a language and literature department.

TABLE 6

ADMINISTRATIVE ORGANIZATION OF THE NDEA LANGUAGE AND AREA CENTERS, AUTUMN, 1960

ORGANIZATION	CENTERS, CLASSIFIED BY AREA					
	African and Luso-Brazilian	Far Eastern (and Far Eastern in Combination with South Asian or Slavic)	Near and Middle Eastern	Slavic, East European, and Uralic-Altaic	South Asian and Southeast Asian	Total
Center consists entirely of a language department (or of a group of language and literature courses)	1	1	1	4	1	8
Core of center is a language department (or a group of language and literature courses), but area courses from other departments are formally connected with center.	1	3	1	2	1	8
Center resides in a single interdisciplinary departmental (or departmentlike) administrative unit containing offerings in both language and area.	. . . . . .	2	1	1	1	5
Center is an interdepartmental enterprise (sometimes tightly and sometimes loosely organized), including language but with stronger orientation to area.	4	7	5	3	6	25
Total.	6	13	8	10	9	46

TABLE 7
AVAILABILITY OF INTERDISCIPLINARY DEGREE OR CERTIFICATE PROGRAMS THROUGH NDEA LANGUAGE AND AREA CENTERS, AUTUMN, 1960

AREA	NUMBER OF CENTERS			B.A.		M.A.		PH.D.		GRADUATE CERTIFICATE ONLY	SUMMARY: GRADUATE DEGREE OR CERTIFICATE
	Graduate	Undergraduate	Total	Major Degree	Minor or Joint Degree *Only*	Major Degree	Minor or Joint Degree *Only*	Major Degree	Minor or Joint Degree *Only*		
African............	4	.....	4	.....	1	1	.....	.....	.....	1	2
Far Eastern........	8	2	10	10	.....	4	1	1*	2	2	8
Far Eastern in combination with South Asian or Slavic...	2	1	3	3	.....	2	.....	1	.....	.....	2
Luso-Brazilian......	2	.....	2	.....	.....	1	.....	1	.....	.....	1
Near and Middle Eastern..........	7	1	8	4	2†	5	1	4*	2	.....	6
Slavic, East European, and Uralic-Altaic...........	10	.....	10	3*	.....	2	1	.....	1	3	6
South Asian and Southeast Asian..	9	.....	9	7	.....	5	1	3*	1	.....	6
Total..........	42	4	46	27	3	20	4	10	6	6	31

* For *one* of the centers listed in each of the rubrics marked with an *, an interdisciplinary degree program is available, but center advisers consider it wiser to major in a single discipline, and candidates are permitted the interdisciplinary program only under unusual circumstances.

† One of these is a certificate program.

TABLE 8

COURSES AND ENROLLMENTS IN THE LANGUAGE PROGRAMS OF NDEA CENTERS, AUTUMN, 1960

LANGUAGE	NUMBER OF CENTERS AT WHICH GIVEN		NUMBER OF LANGUAGE COURSES GIVEN	ENROLLMENTS		
	With Federal Support	Without Federal Support		First-Year Courses	Other Courses	Total
Arabic	8	......	37	110	116	226
Armenian	......	2	3	8	1	9
Bengali	1	......	2	7	6	13
Berber (Shilha)	1	......	1	1	......	1
Burmese	2	......	4	2	4	6
Chinese (Mandarin)	13	......	80	274	403	677
Czech	3	1	6	14	6	20
Estonian	1	......	2	1	1	2
Ethiopic Amharic, Geez, Tigrinya	1	......	2	2	1	3
Finnish	1	......	3	14	3	17
Hebrew	4	2	15	68	89	157
Hindi-Urdu	7	1	23	62	48	110
Hungarian	3	......	7	16	2	18
Indonesian	2	1	7	12	12	24
Japanese	9	1	57	473	485	958
Korean	1	2	7	6	6	12
Kpelle	1	......	1	4	......	4
Lettish	......	1	1	2	......	2
Lithuanian	......	1	1	1	......	1
Marathi	1	......	1	......	1	1
Mongolian	2	1	5	8	4	12
Pali	......	1	1	......	1	1
Persian	6	......	16	20	14	34
Polish	7	......	14	52	39	91
Portuguese	2	......	16	56	70	126
Rumanian	......	1	1	1	......	1
Russian	11	......	170	1,727	2,298	4,025
Sanskrit	......	7	9	51	17	68
Serbo-Croatian	5	1	8	31	7	38
Slovak	1	......	1	6	......	6
Swahili	3	......	6	28	5	33
Tamil	1	......	1	3	......	3
Telugu	3	......	3	6	......	6
Thai	2	......	5	6	8	14
Tibetan	1	1	6	2	12	14
Turkish	6	......	18	27	19	46
Ukrainian	1	......	2	2	......	2
Uralic	......	1	2	6	1	7
Uzbek	1	......	2	2	2	4
Vietnamese	2	......	3	2	2	4
Yoruba	2	......	4	9	3	12
Tutorials in Far Eastern languages	....	....	3	......	24	24
Tutorials in Near Eastern languages	....	....	6	......	12	12
Proseminar in African languages	....	....	1	......	4	4
Seminar in South Asian languages	....	....	1	......	6	6
Total	....	....	564	3,122	3,732	6,854

TABLE 9
NDEA Center Enrollments in Language Courses, Autumn, 1960

Area	Number of Centers	Center Language Enrollment			
		Lowest	Highest	Mean	Total
African..........................	4	4	26	14	54
Far Eastern......................	10	15	634	140	1,402
Far Eastern in Combination with South Asian or Slavic.................	3	41	462	237	711
Luso-Brazilian....................	2	32	95	64	127
Near and Middle Eastern...........	8	9	184	62	498
Slavic, East European, and Uralic-Altaic......................	10	60	689	383	3,831
South Asian and Southeast Asian....	9	8	75	26	231
Total........................	46	......	......	......	6,854
Range........................	....	4	689	149	....

TABLE 10
Number of Centers Offering One or More Intensive Language Courses* during Summer Session, 1960, and Autumn, 1960

Intensive Courses	Centers, Classified by Area					
	African and Luso-Brazilian	Far Eastern (and Far Eastern in Combination with South Asian or Slavic)	Near and Middle Eastern	Slavic, East European, and Uralic-Altaic	South Asian and Southeast Asian	Total
Autumn, 1960						
8 contact hours................	......	3	2	3	3	11
9 contact hours................	......	......	1	......	1	2
10 contact hours.............	2	2	......	3	1	8
30 contact hours.............	......	1	......	......	......	1
Total....................	2	6	3	6	5	22
Summer Session, 1960 (usually at 15 contact hours weekly), but not Autumn, 1960.............	......	2	1	1	2	6
Neither Summer Session, 1960, nor Autumn, 1960..............	4	5	4	3	2	18
Total....................	6	13	8	10	9	46

* "Intensive" is defined for purposes of this table as a language course with eight or more contact hours per week. A large number of the centers offer language courses with six weekly contact hours; these are often referred to in center literature as "intensive" but have not been counted here.

TABLE 11
COMMITMENT TO THE AUDIO-LINGUAL APPROACH IN THE CENTER LANGUAGE
PROGRAMS, AUTUMN, 1960

DEGREE OF COMMITMENT	CENTERS, CLASSIFIED BY AREA					
	African and Luso-Brazilian	Far Eastern (and Far Eastern in Combination with South Asian or Slavic)	Near and Middle Eastern	Slavic, East European, and Uralic-Altaic	South Asian and Southeast Asian	Total
1. There is little concern with audio-lingual principles (or knowledge about them) on the theoretical level; few audio-lingual features were observed in classroom practice..	.....	.....	1	3	.....	4
2. There is little concern or knowledge and/or consistency on the theoretical level, but some audio-lingual features were observed in classroom practice....................	.....	4	1	2	1	8
3. The program is committed to some extent to the audio-lingual approach on the theoretical level; a number of audio-lingual features were observed in classroom practice, but the general approach cannot be described as audio-lingual................	3	2	3	2	1	11
4. The program is largely committed to the audio-lingual approach; yet, while many audio-lingual features were observed in classroom practice and some courses were seen as model examples of this approach, it is not dominant in center practice........	2	3	1	1	4	11
5. The program is fully committed to the audio-lingual approach on the theoretical level, and it is dominant in center practice.	1	4	2	2	3	12
Total...............................	6	13	8	10	9	46

TABLE 12
LANGUAGE LABORATORIES AT LANGUAGE AND AREA CENTERS, AUTUMN, 1960

LABORATORY FACILITIES	CENTERS, CLASSIFIED BY AREA					
	African and Luso-Brazilian	Far Eastern (and Far Eastern in Combination with South Asian or Slavic)	Near and Middle Eastern	Slavic, East European, and Uralic-Altaic	South Asian and Southeast Asian	Total
1a. There is no laboratory at the center....	....	......	2	....	.....	2
1b. There is no laboratory at the center but one is under construction or planned for the immediate future............	2	3	....	.....	1	6
2a. There are very limited laboratory facilities (or limited use of facilities belonging to another department)..........	.....	1	....	......	.....	1
2b. There are very limited laboratory facilities but a laboratory is under construction or planned for the immediate future................................	.....	1	1	1	3	6
3. A laboratory is available to center students, tapes are prepared for them, and they are encouraged to use these facilities. But the laboratory is not an integral part of the center program*......	3	4	1	5	3	16
4. There are good or excellent laboratory facilities available to center students and laboratory work is an integral part of the language program............	1	4	4	4	2	15
Total...........................	6	13	8	10	9	46

* Because of lack of facilities or machines, or lack of concern and/or knowledge on the part of the staff.

TABLE 13

RELATIONSHIP BETWEEN COMMITMENT TO THE AUDIO-LINGUAL APPROACH AND USE OF THE LABORATORY AT NDEA LANGUAGE AND AREA CENTERS, AUTUMN, 1960

CLASSIFICATION OF CENTERS WITH RESPECT TO AUDIO-LINGUAL COMMITMENT IN ACCORDANCE WITH CATEGORIES OF TABLE 11	CLASSIFICATION OF CENTERS WITH RESPECT TO LABORATORY USE IN ACCORDANCE WITH CATEGORIES OF TABLE 12			TOTAL
	Categories 1 and 2 No Laboratory or Very Limited Facilities	Category 3 Laboratory Available and Encouraged	Category 4 Laboratory Work Integrated with Program	
Categories 4 and 5 Center fully or largely committed to the audio-lingual approach.................	5	7	11	23
Categories 1, 2, and 3 Center committed to the audio-lingual approach to some extent or not at all............	10	9	4	23
Total number of centers.....	15	16	15	46

TABLE 14

COURSE OFFERINGS IN AREA AT NDEA LANGUAGE AND AREA CENTERS, AUTUMN, 1960

AREA	COURSE OFFERINGS											
	Anthropology and Sociology	Economics	Education	Geography	History	Linguistics	Literature,* the Arts, and History of Culture	Philosophy and Religion	Political Science	Science	Interdisciplinary Courses	Total
African..............	8	2	2	4	5	2	....	....	2	...	3	28
Far Eastern..........	10	7	1	7	52	5	49	8	27	2	58	226
Luso-Brazilian........	11	3	...	4	8	5	2	....	4	...	2	39
Near and Middle Eastern...............	6	4	...	5	25	8	3	1	8	...	20	80
Slavic, East European, and Uralic-Altaic....	8	13	1	8	39	6	55	3	37	...	6	176
South Asian and Southeast Asian..........	15	4	2	5	13	1	13	17	16	...	12	98
Total............	58	33	6	33	142	27	122	29	94	2	101	647

* Literature courses appear on this list only if given in English; literature courses in which the foreign language is the medium of instruction appear in the language course offerings listed in Table 8.

TABLE 15

STUDENTS	African (N=4)	Far Eastern (N=13)	Luso-Brazilian (N=2)	Near and Middle Eastern (N=8)	Slavic, East European, and Uralic-Altaic (N=12)	South Asian and Southeast Asian (N=10)	Total
Majors and minors for the B.A. degree	....	247	1	82	129	10	469
Majors and minors for the M.A. degree	8	70	3	62	196	38	377
Majors and minors for either the M.A. or Ph.D. degree†	....	129	3	9	131	59	331
Majors and minors for the Ph.D. degree	35	149	.....	80	208	115	587
Majors and minors for a graduate certificate‡	1	3	.....	.....	120	.....	124
Total graduate majors and minors	44	351	6	151	655	212	1,419
Special graduate students (including postdoctoral students)	....	.....	.....	3	67	2	72
Total	44	598	7	236	851	224	1,960

Centers, Classified by Area*

* The number of centers shown under Far Eastern includes two in Far Eastern and Slavic, but only the majors and minors in the Far Eastern programs at those centers are counted in the figures under Far Eastern; their Slavic majors and minors are counted in the figures under Slavic. The same treatment has been given to the one other center operating in two areas, Far Eastern and South Asian.

† We have had to adopt this category because our data for some of the centers tell us only the number of graduate majors and minors, without differentiating between those in M.A. programs and those in Ph.D. programs.

‡ A certificate major is often an M.A. candidate simultaneously, but typically the M.A. degree will not be taken through the center or one of its constituent parts.

TABLE 16

NUMBER OF GRADUATE STUDENTS AT NDEA LANGUAGE AND AREA CENTERS
HOLDING SCHOLARSHIPS OR FELLOWSHIPS FOR LANGUAGE STUDY,
AUTUMN, 1960

TYPE OF SCHOLARSHIP OR FELLOWSHIP	CENTERS, CLASSIFIED BY AREA							
	African	Far Eastern	Far Eastern in Combination with Slavic or South Asian	Luso-Brazilian	Near and Middle Eastern	Slavic, East European, and Uralic-Altaic	South Asian and Southeast Asian	TOTAL
University fellowship or scholarship	14*	15	. . . . . .	. . . . . .	21	34	12	96
NDEA fellowship	7	59	41	20	29	95	50	301
Ford fellowship	15	7	3	. . . . . .	9	28	24	86
Fellowships from other foundations	6	3	1	. . . . . .	4	25	13	52
State fellowship or scholarship	. . . . . .	3	. . . . . .	. . . . . .	. . . . . .	53	. . . . . .	56
Other	. . . . . .	1	. . . . . .	. . . . . .	1	. . . . . .	. . . . . .	2
Total	42	88	45	20	64	235	99	593

* Teaching and research assistants have not been included in these figures; but in this one case, university research assistants and university fellowship holders were reported together as a single figure.

Conference Participants

At each of the five conferences called for representatives of the NDEA centers by the American Council on Education, the project director served as recorder (and was responsible for the conference report) and the associate director served as discussion chairman. The center representatives at each of the conferences are given in the following list.

Conference I: For Representatives of South Asia and Southeast Asia Language and Area Centers
San Francisco, California, March 2–3, 1961

South Asia

University of Arizona: J. Michael Mahar, Bernard S. Silberman
University of California, Berkeley: John J. Gumperz, Leo Rose
University of Chicago: Edward Dimock, Myron Weiner
Cornell University: Gordon H. Fairbanks, Murray A. Straus
University of Pennsylvania: W. Norman Brown, Richard D. Lambert
University of Texas: Winfred P. Lehmann, James R. Roach
University of Wisconsin: Henry C. Hart, Gerald B. Kelley

Southeast Asia

Cornell University: John M. Echols
University of Hawaii: Samuel H. Elbert, John White
Yale University: Harry J. Benda, William Cornyn

Special guest: Richard Park, University of Michigan

Conference II: For Representatives of Slavic and East European Language and Area Centers
International House, Chicago, Illinois, March 10–11, 1961

University of California, Berkeley: Lawrence L. Thomas, Francis J. Whitfield
University of Colorado: S. Harrison Thomson, Serge A. Zenkovsky
Columbia University: William Harkins, Henry L. Roberts
Fordham University: Rev. W. C. Jaskievicz, S.J., Anthony Vasys

Harvard University: Mrs. S. Pirkova-Yakobson, V. Setschkareff
University of Illinois: Ralph T. Fisher, Jr., Ralph E. Matlaw
Indiana University: Robert F. Byrnes, William B. Edgerton
University of Michigan: William B. Ballis, Deming Brown
University of Pennsylvania: Alexander V. Riasanovsky, Alfred Senn
University of Southern California: Alexander Kosloff, Roger Swearingen
University of Washington: Victor Erlich, Laurence C. Thompson

Conference III: For Representatives of African and Luso-Brazilian Language and Area Centers
Washington, D.C., March 13–14, 1961

Africa

University of California, Los Angeles: Benjamin E. Thomas, William Welmers

Duquesne University: Geza Grosschmid, Rev. Henry J. Lemmens, C.S.Sp.

Howard University: Priscilla C. Reining, Mark Hanna Watkins

Michigan State University: Eugene Jacobson, Hans Wolff

Luso-Brazilian Area

New York University: Ernesto Guerra Da Cal, Carleton Sprague Smith

University of Wisconsin: Alberto Machado da Rosa, William P. Glade, Jr.

Special guests: Maurice Albertson, Melvin Fox

Also present at the opening session of this conference were Arthur S. Adams and Harrison Sasscer, of the American Council on Education; George Faust, Louise Howe, Elsa Liles, and Judith LeBovit, of the U.S. Office of Education; and Herman R. Allen, of the Inventory staff.

Conference IV: For Representatives of Near and Middle East Language and Area Centers
International House, Chicago, Illinois, April 10–11, 1961

University of California, Los Angeles: Andreas Tietze, G. E. von Grunebaum

Harvard University: D. W. Lockard, William R. Polk
Johns Hopkins University: Wilson Bishai, Yousif Fargo
University of Michigan: George Cameron, George Grassmuck
Portland State College: Frederick J. Cox, George Hoffmann
Princeton University: Lewis V. Thomas, Farhat J. Ziadeh
University of Texas: W. Lehn, Wolfgang Lentz
University of Utah: Frederick P. Latimer, William Mulder

Special guest: Wolf Leslau, University of California, Los Angeles

*Conference V: For Representatives of Far Eastern
Language and Area Centers
Denver, Colorado, April 13–14, 1961*

University of Arizona: Don C. Bailey, Bernard S. Silberman
University of Chicago: E. A. Kracke, Jr., Edwin McClellan
Columbia University: W. Theodore de Bary, Ichiro I. Shirato
Cornell University: Harriet C. Mills, Robert J. Smith
Harvard University: James R. Hightower, Rulan C. Pian
University of Hawaii: Ronald S. Anderson, Yukuo Uyehara
State University of Iowa: Ramon L. Y. Woon
University of Kansas: Thomas R. Smith, Benjamin Wallacker
University of Michigan: Richard K. Beardsley, Joseph K. Yamagiwa
University of Pittsburgh: Samuel C. Chu, Wu-chi Liu
University of Southern California: Theodore H. E. Chen, Roger Swearin-
    gen
Stanford University: Shau Wing Chan, Nobutaka Ike
University of Washington: Richard N. McKinnon, Turrell V. Wylie

Special guest: Frederick J. Cox, Portland State College, Undergraduate
    Center Representative

AMERICAN COUNCIL ON EDUCATION

LOGAN WILSON, *President*

The American Council on Education is a *council* of national educational associations; organizations having related interests; approved universities, colleges, teachers colleges, junior colleges, technological schools, and selected private secondary schools; state departments of education; city school systems and private school systems; selected educational departments of business and industrial companies; voluntary associations of higher education in the states; and large public libraries. It is a center of cooperation and coordination whose influence has been apparent in the shaping of American educational policies and the formation of educational practices during the past forty-four years.